American Lake VIGNETTES

NANCY COVERT

Charleston London
THE History PRESS

Published by The History Press
Charleston, SC 29403
www.historypress.net

First published 2014

Manufactured in the United States

ISBN 978.1.62619.270.6

Library of Congress CIP data applied for.

CONTENTS

CONTENTS

CONTENTS

FISHING ON THE LAKE

No one could have predicted how important those days at the lake would prove to the boy. It was a case of lifelong love that proved to be a significant factor in his lengthy life.

—*Louis Raphael,* They're in There

They're in there," says Louis Raphael, who fished American Lake in the 1940s. In his 2009 memoir, *They're in There: A Life on American Lake*, Tacoma author Louis Raphael tells about the summer he was fourteen and came to the lake to help his grandfather John Seidelman, who managed Don Gawley's Boathouse at Tillicum on American Lake. Gawley had originally purchased Garrison's Resort, as the enterprise first was known. Mr. Raphael, a retired journalism teacher, is also a retired *News Tribune* writer.

In the 1940s, Bill Merritt made an offer for the business, and Gawley accepted, according to Raphael. Although Glenn Anderson bought the business in 1971, the boathouse is still known as "Bill's" and features a towering carved wood statue of Bill the fisherman.

Louis's salary during those summers was forty dollars a month, plus room and board in a shack on the dock.

"But the perks included a girl on the diving board, a pair of dogs—Butch and Chubby—a commando raid, and a deaf Scotsman," Louis recalled. And a book chock-full of fine memories from those unforgettable summers he spent fishing on the big, beautiful lake.

Mr. Raphael's easy-to-read memoir reels the reader in with the lazy but comforting retelling of his own Tom Sawyer–like adventures spent on the largest of the area's dozen lakes, formed by a receding glacier thousands of years ago. Louis knows from firsthand experience that "they're in there."

With Louis's permission, here are a few excerpts from his memoir:

What? Me Pay?

> *Of course, I got spoiled with free boat rental for years as a perk of my employment and, I guess, a kind of retirement bonus, from Grandpa. It has always gone against the grain with me to pay to rent a boat. Grandpa remained at his employment at the boathouse for a few years after Paul and I worked for him. He was eventually booted out, and a guy named Bert Thomas, a long-distance swimmer of some note, ran the boathouse for a while. Sometime later a man named Anderson* [Glenn] *took over and provided service until his death. His family* [Dave Anderson, now president of the Tillicum/Woodbrook Neighborhood Association and editor of a weekly newsletter for Tillicum/Woodbrook residents] *still operates the boathouse.*

"But the boat rental business is barely alive today," Raphael continues. Firch's has long since folded. There was a boat rental business for years on the western shore near the seaplane base (closed shortly after the start of the twenty-first century).

> *I kept my homemade boat there for a year or two when I was a young teacher, and I fished almost every summer morning before breakfast. When I came home to my place in Lakewood, I usually had fish.*
>
> *As near as I can figure it without going into convulsions, I fished for 63 years in American Lake. There were some times when "class failures" and getting skunked multiple times in a row made me take a holiday from the lake, but I always came back.*
>
> *In later years I was in touch with my* [boyhood] *friend Jim Hutson. I played slow pitch baseball for his team, and we had lunch together a time or two. Jim said he never fished in American Lake anymore, even though his office was in Tillicum. He was busy with baseball, football and basketball, as both player and coach.*

But I stuck with American even through lean years when, as one super friendly black man I encountered near the boathouse said all he had caught that year were "ring-tailed perch." I am still thinking about that one.

As near as I can figure I started fishing in American Lake in 1942 and fished there at least once every year through 2005. Some of my friends have been married nearly that long—and to one person. But I got along with the lake better than any woman I ever knew, even though I felt it was trying to drown me a time or two.

After all these years, American Lake is still the lake of my dreams. If it were any better it would be too perfect.

What a break to have such an experience during my formative years. Those days on our big raft of a dock must surely have rivaled those of Mark Twain's characters on the Mississippi.

I still dream from time to time of fishing with Jim, or alone. The lake is American, and I know they're in there. I am always hoping to feel once more that pulsing on my rod that pleases so much. You might even say I got a few.

ACKNOWLEDGEMENTS

Twenty years from now, you will be more disappointed by the things that you didn't do than by the ones you did do, so throw off the bowlines, sail away from the safe harbor. Catch the trade winds in your sails. Explore. Dream. Discover.
—Mark Twain

Completing this book, *American Lake Vignettes*, reinforced a personal belief about the value of history, particularly local history. Throughout the two-year project, not only did I learn more about the new community to which I relocated, but I also gained many new acquaintances along the way, including Louis, Jim, Virginia, David, Bob and Susan, as well as Diane, Gloria, Carol, Jack, Art and others, from both sides of the lake.

Big "thanks" to Becky Huber, of the Lakewood Historical Society, for her encouragement, and also to Steilacoom resident Milt Davidson for loaning his personal collection of "the Log" and others who shared their stories for this project.

To learn more about Lake City and Tillicum, as well as side trips to Camp Murray and Fort Lewis (now known as Joint Base Lewis-McChord), I invested many interesting hours reading through materials archived at the Tacoma Public Library's Northwest Room, so a big thanks goes to Brian Kamens; thanks also to Michael Sullivan, University of Washington–Tacoma history professor/Tacoma's former historic preservation officer; to the late Murray Morgan, Tacoma historian extraordinaire; to Louis Raphael IV of Tacoma for sharing his American Lake fishing memoir; to Virginia Maas for sharing her writing experiences; and also to the multitude of Lake City and Tillicum residents, past and present, who shared their recollections and photos for this project.

Special thanks to Elizabeth Parkinson, whose mother, Mrs. James (Rose) Parkinson, was the Lake City Community Club's secretary (1957–58) and an amateur historian. It was the discovery of a 1961 newspaper article that sparked the search that came to fruition in May 2014. More than fifty years earlier, Rose had planned to compile a history of the community and attempted to uncover specific details about the early days of the one-room school. She and Mrs. Nelson hoped residents with more information would contact them.

According to Elizabeth, her mother eventually presented a short paper about the history she'd researched during one of the club meetings in the 1960s. This book is also dedicated to Mrs. Parkinson and the many residents around American Lake who dreamed about a local history book.

INTRODUCTION

Aside from Salt Lake City, Utah, which is the largest "lake city" community on any U.S. lake, there are fifteen other lake city communities across the country. Ranging from Utah's sea gull–populated inland sea to tiny Lake City in Marshall County, South Dakota, measuring 128 acres and with a population of fifty-one residents, lake cities have long embodied residents' dreams of living near water.

In Washington State, there are eight thousand lakes, but only two communities are named "Lake City," one on Lake Washington and one on American Lake. Lake City North is a Seattle suburb, while Lake City South is a neighborhood of the City of Lakewood.

Other "Lake City" communities are located in Florida, Minnesota (founded in 1680), Texas, California, Nevada, Pennsylvania, Maine, Tennessee, Illinois, Indiana, Georgia and South Carolina.

In the later years of the nineteenth century, Tacoma's entrepreneurs had plans to make the region's largest lake, American Lake, its playground for the 1872 City of Destiny, complete with rail access.

In May 1889, an area south of American Lake actually had a larger impact on Tacoma's history after the former prairie lands were transformed into a staging area for military operations in the Northwest. By 1917, that area had become Fort Lewis, the location for the Northwest's premier military post.

England's Lakes District versus Lakewood's "Lakes District"

While the area south of Tacoma long has been known as the "Lakes District" (with twelve lakes), there is another famous Lake District across the pond in England. That region contains nineteen lakes.

England's Lake District, also commonly known as the Lakes or (particularly as an adjective) Lakeland, is a mountainous region in northwest England. A popular holiday destination, it is famous not only for its lakes, forests and mountains (or *fells*) but also for its associations with the early nineteenth-century poetry and writings of William Wordsworth and the other Lake Poets.

Historically shared by the counties of Cumberland, Westmorland and Lancashire, the Lake District lies entirely within the modern county of Cumbria. All the land in England higher than three thousand feet above sea level lies within the national park, including Scafell Pike, England's highest mountain. It also contains Wastwater and Windermere, the deepest and longest lakes in England.

Britain's Lake District National Park includes nearly all of the Lake District, though the town of Kendal and the Lakeland Peninsulas are currently outside the park boundary.

The area, which was designated a national park on May 9, 1951 (less than a month after the Peaks District, the first United Kingdom national park designation), is the most visited national park in the United Kingdom (with 15.8 million annual visitors and more than 23.0 million annual day visitors), the largest of the thirteen National Parks in England and Wales and the second largest in the UK after the Cairngorms. Its aim is to protect the landscape by restricting unwelcome change by industry or commerce. Most of the land in the park is in private ownership. The National Trust owns about a quarter of the total area (including some lakes and land of significant landscape value), United Utilities owns 8.0 percent and 3.9 percent belongs to the Lake District National Park Authority.

In common with all other National Parks in England, there is no restriction on entry to, or movement within, the park along public routes, but access to cultivated land is usually restricted to public footpaths.

These lakes and mountains combine to form impressive scenery. The region's ecology has been modified by humans for more than a millennium. Farmland and settlements add aesthetic value to the natural scenery of an area that includes important wildlife habitats.

INTRODUCTION

After residing for two decades in "the first" Pierce County community, where its residents are well aware of the area's important role in the history of its country and state, I "set sail" for something worthwhile to do after retiring. Although I didn't sail far from my adopted hometown of Steilacoom, I soon discovered that my new home wasn't as focused on its history as the former (Steilacoom had been established more than a century earlier).

When I began my quest to learn about American Lake's history, I was told that there wasn't any formal history about the area. Why not research it and write a book?

So the search began, and along the way, assisted by many area residents, I uncovered numerous little-known aspects about the two communities on opposite sides of the largest lake in the region.

It all began when Allen C. Mason and a pair of realtors began promoting American Lake as Tacoma's "playground." While American Lake realized neither Mason's dreams nor the extravagant plans of its other investors for the area to become Tacoma's primary recreational site for very long, today the communities around the lake are two of several "bedroom communities" for the City of Lakewood (incorporated in 1996). At this writing, Lake City (the oldest lakeside community) remains the focus for many water-related recreational activities.

Traces of Lake City's 125-year-old beginning can be found at various places around the lake, from Lake City Community Church and the American Lake Veterans Affairs Hospital on the west side to with Thornewood Castle and Bill's Boathouse on the east side and elsewhere around this glacier-formed lake.

I'm hopeful that others will find these nuggets of history as interesting as I did, and I encourage/challenge them to uncover those little gems that Louis knows are "still in there."

Chapter 1

COOL WATERS

The Ice Sheet that Formed Washington's Lakes District

American Lake: Two miles southwest of Lake View, on the Olympia branch of the N.P. Railroad. Eleven miles from the courthouse. Mail Lakeview R.F.D. Voting precinct: American Lake.
—Settlements of the County in History of Pierce County,
by W.P. Bonney, 1927

What was it about American Lake that attracted the attention of Tacoma's nineteenth-century businessmen to the point where they decided that the area around the lake would make an ideal "playground" for them? Even though Tacoma, by that time, was starting to develop Point Defiance, that regional park didn't offer the same opportunities that American Lake did.

Although American Lake never achieved the dreams of its earliest promoters, such as Allen C. Mason and others, it came closer than any other early city plans toward fulfilling their "playground" ideals.

The Mountain that Was God: Mount Rainier/Mount Tacoma

"The mountain," as most Washingtonians today refer to the large, white, ice cream sundae–shaped mountain east of American Lake, is a prominent state icon and featured on numerous items from stationery and postage stamps to T-shirts and candy bars. Located in Pierce County, the mountain is the focal point of Mount Rainier National Park, established in 1899.

On a clear day, its expansive, white-cloaked splendor languishes majestically across the landscape. One never tires of seeing it. For first-time viewers, it's understandable why they might think that American Lake's waters originated from the mountain, but that's not the case.

Viewed in 1792 by British captain George Vancouver during his exploration of the Puget Sound region, the mountain's Native American name of *Tacoma* was changed to honor his friend Rear Admiral Peter Rainier. That naming decision led to disputes that lasted more than three hundred years. Ultimately, the natives settled on the Rainier name, explaining that they would always consider it to be Tacoma/Tacobet no matter what.

The Native Americans called it *Talol* or *Tacoma* or *Tahoma*, from the Lushootseed word *təqʷúʔbəʔ*, or "mother of waters," as spoken by the Puyallups. Another definition is that *Tacoma* means "larger than Mount Baker." American explorers Lewis and Clark, on their 1804–6 journey, referred to it as "Mount Regniere."

In Theodore Winthrop's posthumously published 1862 travel book, *The Canoe and the Saddle*, he referred to the mountain as "Tacoma," and for a time, both names were used interchangeably, although "Mount Tacoma" was preferred in the city of Tacoma.

Rainier is the highest mountain in Washington and in the Cascade Range. It has a topographic prominence of 14,410 feet. K2, the world's second-tallest mountain, is twice as high as Rainier.

Rising from the Nisqually Plain, inland from Puget Sound, Mount Rainier is a 235,615-acre national park that was established at the end of the nineteenth century. It is part of the Cascade Range and is visible throughout the region.

On clear days, it dominates the southeastern horizon in most of the Seattle-Tacoma metropolitan area to such an extent that locals sometimes refer to it simply as "the Mountain." On days of exceptional clarity, it also can be seen from as far away as Portland, Oregon, and Victoria, British Columbia.

With twenty-six major glaciers—including the Carbon, Puyallup, Mowich and Nisqually—and thirty-six square miles (ninety-three square kilometers) of permanent snowfields and glaciers, Mount Rainier is the most heavily glaciated peak in the lower forty-eight states. Two volcanic craters top the summit, each more than one thousand feet (three hundred meters) in diameter with the larger east crater overlapping the west crater.

The sleeping volcano's geothermal heat keeps areas of both crater rims free of snow and ice and contains the world's largest volcanic glacier cave network within the ice-filled craters, with nearly two miles of passages. A small crater lake, about 130 by 30 feet and 16 feet deep (with a surface elevation of 14,203 feet, the highest in North America), occupies the lowest portion of the west crater, below more than 100 feet of ice, and is accessible only via the caves.

By 1890, the United States Board on Geographic Names declared that the mountain would be known as "Rainier." Following this, in 1897, the Pacific Forest Reserve became the Mount Rainier Forest Reserve, and the national park was established two years later. Despite this, there was still a movement to change the mountain's name to "Tacoma," and as late as 1924, Congress was still considering a resolution to change the name. Periodically, the mountain's "rightful" name still comes up for debate.

American Lake's Formation

Nearly all lakes in the Puget Sound Basin, from sea level to timberline, are the products of glacial processes, according to professor Arthur Krukeberg in his definitive book *The Natural History of Puget Sound Country*.

At low elevations, the last continental ice sheet (Vashon Glacier—about fourteen thousand years ago) gouged depressions out of preexisting alluvial deposits to form the basins that would fill with water as the ice melted or receded.

Many lakes of the south Puget areas near the terminus of the great Vashon ice sheet were formed by detached blocks of ice mixed with sand and gravel, which became stranded and, after melting, formed the depressions called "kettles" (Lake Louise, Lake Waughop and Carp Lake are kettle lakes, for example).

As the ice receded, the melting water and large boulders embedded within the ice scraped the ground beneath, leaving barren lands. The prairie that in the early twentieth century became the Lake City/Tillicum area was created this way. A large portion of this prairie came under the jurisdiction of the British Hudson's Bay Company, through an organization called the Puget Sound Agricultural Company, managed by Joseph Heath until the Americans' arrival.

The area in which American Lake was located was part of the 161,295-acre "farm" owned by the Puget Sound Agricultural Company. When the British left the area, the United States government paid $650,000 to the Hudson's Bay Company for the land.

In his *Memoirs of Nisqually—1845–49*, Heath recorded in his journal, dated Sunday, June 13, 1847: "Rode out around the Great Lake [probably American Lake]. Found only one deer at which I got a shot, but missed. It would have broken cover close to me, had it not been frightened by my white trousers."

American Lake at 1,100 acres, with a per-acre-foot volume of sixty thousand gallons of water, is the largest (three miles long with twelve miles of shoreline) in an area that contains a dozen lakes, including Gravelly, Steilacoom, Louise and Waughop. The lake is about 105 feet in depth, while Gravelly Lake measures about 160 feet in depth. After the last of the ice melted, these prairie lands were ready for the next chapter in this majestic ongoing drama.

According to one early explanation, since dismissed by twenty-first-century hydrologists, the stream's (Clover Creek) rising in spring was believed to be influenced by the vast underground flow of water through the bed of gravel that lies between the melting snows of Mount Tacoma and the Sound.

These assorted lakes are in an area known as the Lakes District, not to be confused with England's northern Lake District. The City of Lakewood, established in 1996, is the largest metropolitan community south of Tacoma, but that wasn't always the case.

Spootslith or American? Who Named the Lake?

It was considered a true Eden—shining waters and abundant plants and game awaited the first inhabitants who occupied the lands for hundreds of years until the late eighteenth century.

Long before the white men arrived in the area, the largest lake in the Lakes District was called "Spootslith" by the native inhabitants.

"The lake was included in Steilacoom tribal territory," wrote Danny Marshall, Steilacoom tribal council chairman, in the tribe's spring 2013 newsletter.

In an early twentieth-century article published in 1916 by *Tacoma Daily Ledger* editor Herb Hunt ("History of Pierce County: Its People and Its History"), he recorded the story told by Slugamus Coquilton, an Indian, who "used to say that American Lake had borne that name" since the Wilkes party celebrated the Fourth of July at Sequalitchew in 1841. It has long been the belief that Captain (also called Lieutenant) Wilkes named it, probably combining a patriotic impulse and a desire to honor Mrs. America Richmond, wife of John Richmond, the Methodist missionary at the Hudson's Bay Company post in 1840–42.

American Lake. *Author's collection.*

Wilkes was the commander of the American Exploratory Expedition (1838–42) that explored and mapped the waters of the inland Northwest, including Puget Sound, and Antarctica. While visiting the Hudson's Bay Company fort at Nisqually, it was claimed that Wilkes and his shipmates celebrated the "first" Fourth of July near American Lake.

Even the Brits joined in the celebration.

Trappers and explorers followed after the Native Americans, and when the British Hudson's Bay Company established its south Puget Sound headquarters at the mouth of Sequalitchew Creek, hundreds of white settlers followed, intending to establish an American foothold on the property.

Fort Nisqually at Point Defiance Park in Tacoma is an authentic replica of the Hudson's Bay Company palisade that was constructed first in 1833 and then again in the early 1840s on higher ground along the Sequalitchew Creek. In 1933, parts of the fort were relocated to the park site. *Library of Congress.*

Despite the impressive view of Mount Tahoma rising in the distance at the lake's northeastern end, there is no truth to the belief that the melting glacial waters from the mountain filled the lakes—nor is there any truth to a more recent rumor that early twentieth-century Pierce County entrepreneur Norton Clapp was responsible for dredging 320 acres of Lake Steilacoom, although he was responsible for developing other prominent projects in the area, such as the Lakewood Community Center, now known as the Lakewood Colonial Center, and the Ice Arena, as well as being a partner in the Paragon Corporation, which built the Space Needle for the 1962 World's Fair.

Seventy-five years after Captain Charles Wilkes led his marines in a celebration of the first American Fourth of July on the plains of American Lake, known by its Native American name of Spootslith, a group of 150 Tacoma businessmen presented a petition to the Board of Pierce County Commissioners asking them to call a special election to authorize the issuance of $2 million in bonds for purchasing the American Lake site for a cantonment.

There have been several explanations about how American Lake received its name, all from accounts that tell about Captain Wilkes and Reverend Richmond naming the lake.

Historian Edmund S. Meany of the University of Washington, in his *Origins of Washington Geographic Names*, writes, "There is a persistent error as to the origin of this name [American Lake]. The error declares that the name arose from the fact that the Wilkes Expedition celebrated the Fourth of July 1841 on the shore of the lake and thus contributed to its name."

This is very beautiful but, according to Meany, "not true." Meany said that the Wilkes narrative does not even mention the lake, "the place of that national celebration was on the edge of Mission Prairie, and the men were landed from the ships [west of the fort] and marched to the place, about a mile distant."

Meany also notes in his book that, according to Mrs. Mary Frost, she moved in 1854 into a cabin on a donation claim near the lake. Other American settlers, such as the Bonneys, had claims in the area, and the name "American" undoubtedly grew from that fact, since the British still held the ground around Fort Nisqually.

Meanwhile, the Indian name for the lake was "Spootals," one derived from an interesting legend. The east end of the lake is narrow. Deer, when hard pressed, swam across it here, followed by hunters, if they were daring enough. At great intervals, and seen only by the select, the water suddenly would begin a movement that produced a great whirlpool, causing a musical swishing sound. Then there would appear, as if caused by the rushing waters, a beautiful striped horse called Spootals or Spootslith.

Any hunter who saw the Spootals, even if only for an instant, in time became great and usually was elevated to a chief's role.

Who Were the Original Owners of the Land?

Ownership of the lands now occupied by Joint Base Lewis-McChord (JBLM) has long been disputed. E-mail correspondence between the author and Danny Marshall outlined the dilemma:

> *The recognized boundary between the Steilacoom and Nisqually is the Nisqually River. I believe that all of Ft. Lewis falls North of the Nisqually river. Therefore, it is safe to say that the Steilacoom people were the owners and occupants of all of Joint Base Lewis McChord (JBLM) area. One of the reasons that our people were impacted heavily by Fort Lewis is that without a reservation most of the families settled on land that was condemned and taken from them when the military reservation was established. Fort Lewis was not the*

positive impact for my people that it was planned to be for Pierce County. We did not get a reservation in 1854–56 due to the first American town (Steilacoom) being in our area, and when we moved to other traditional village areas we lost our land again at the establishment of Fort Lewis. The US Government should surplus unused military reservation areas back to the authority of the Steilacoom Tribe; this would be the correct thing to do.

This was an important factor in the Federal Acknowledgement case for the Steilacoom Tribe. Bottom line is that the U.S. Government decided to start not recognizing the landless tribes in the 1950's. Prior to this all the tribes were treated the same. Now if you don't have a reservation you aren't recognized; bad news for us. In the acknowledgement review there is a criteria that looks at tribal families living together in groups or communities. Many of the people on the rolls today (including my family) all lived together in lands on North Fort Lewis.

When we lost that land, we were forced to move around again, which further dispersed us. Even though the majority of our people still live in traditional tribal areas of Pierce County, there is not a large pocket of families in a single community—this is a negative tick in the federal acknowledgement clock of injustice.

According to notes from *The Nisqually Tribe*, by Robert H. Ruby and John A. Brown (University of Oklahoma Press, 1992):

On Sept. 30, 1884, the acreage set aside for the Nisqually Reservation was divided into 30 allotments on both sides of the river; it did not include the river itself. Tribal members received few government rations, and among other foods they consumed 500 salmon annually per family. In the winter of 1917, the U.S. Army, without warning, moved onto Nisqually lands and ordered them from their homes. The army later condemned about ⅔ (3,353 acres of the Nisqually Reservation) to expand its Camp Lewis here.

Sherwood Bonney, an Early Settler, Files His Claim

Sherwood Bonney was born on February 18, 1812, in Cornwall, Connecticut. His family relocated the following year to Ohio, settling in Portage County. After his father died and his mother remarried, Sherwood struck out on his own. In 1837, Sherwood married Elizabeth Byrnes, and in 1839, they moved to Iowa. In the spring of 1852, they joined one of the westward-heading wagon trains, starting on April 7, 1852, from Council Bluffs. The wagon train was so large that it took four days for the crossing—with the last wagon crossing on the final day.

"There was neither comfort by day nor rest by night," Sherwood remarked.

The wagon train finally reached Oregon and remained there for several months. In February 1853, after the death of his first wife, Elizabeth, he married Lydia, his brother's widow, uniting their two families before heading north to Steilacoom, where they spent a couple nights with the DeVores at a site to which they later returned. Sherwood then filed a donation claim for 322.90 acres along American Lake (Sections 16 and 17, Twp. 19, Range 2 East).

In later years, Sherwood's daughter Mary Bonney Shorey recalled the beauty of their American Lake homestead, particularly the abundance of wildflowers, such as wood violets, in the spring. In William P. Bonney's *History of Pierce County*, Mary said, "Father and mother took advantage of the 'Oregon Donation Land Law' and filed on 320 acres of land bordering on American Lake, one of the beauty spots of Pierce County, three miles from Steilacoom."

It was a veritable park. The shores of the lake were fringed with wild roses, and underneath the spreading oak trees, the violets and buttercups made a dainty and beautiful carpet. A good six-room house was built with two fireplaces, in which a fire of oak logs blazed cheerfully, as needed.

"Having several teams of oxen," Mary said, "Father and the older boys did much work for the neighbors, thus earning funds to help provide for the large family." Mary, who was eight at that time, recalled taking her infant sister in a cart to Steilacoom from their American Lake home to take shelter because of an imminent Indian attack.

At one point in Sherwood's long life in this county, he is credited with damming the water flow from a series of ponds for Andrew Byrd's mill, eventually transforming the ponds into what today is known as Lake Steilacoom.

During their stay in Steilacoom, Mrs. Bonney served as the first teacher for the school district that was established in 1854. The small DeVore cabin was the setting for the first class of twenty-seven students, seven of whom were Bonney children.

Bonney served as the first justice of the peace to be elected by voters and presided over the first marriage conducted by a civil officer. His justice of the peace duties took him around the county, and eventually he settled in a community above Sumner, where the Bonney name was bestowed on another Pierce County lake that today retains that connection.

Sherwood died on March 30, 1908, at age ninety-six in Sumner and is buried in the Sumner Cemetery on East Valley Road. The Bonneys' youngest son, William, eventually compiled a comprehensive, three-volume set titled *History of Pierce County*, published in 1927.

American Lake or Lake Britannica? The *Log*'s Opinion

American Lake, the Lakes District's largest lake (out of twelve), might have been named Lake Britannica, according to speculation by *Lakewood Log* publisher Charles Mann. Fortunately, in the "diplomatic victory gained by the United States in the Treaty of 1846, the boundary between Britain [now Canada] and America was established at the 49th Parallel, and all that remains of the former British presence is the now-historic recreated Hudson's Bay headquarters of Ft. Nisqually located at Pt. Defiance."

Mann wrote the following opinion in his 1959 description of early aspirations for Lake City:

> *Then in 1889, Lake City, Washington Territory, was platted. It came into being as a main line railroad, but Fate decided otherwise.*
>
> *The Lake City Land Co., headed by Frank C. Ross, C.A.E. Naubert and Fremont Campbell offered lots for sale at $50 to $100. They advertised about carriages always ready to show this property. The Tacoma and Lake City Land and Navigation Company was formed, and a railroad line was built between North Union and 26th St. and ran through Oakland, Flett, Park Lodge and Sherwood to Lake City.*
>
> *The road was Standard Gauge because they planned to continue the line from American Lake to the Sound and down through Olympia to Oregon. The approaches to the bridge that later became the Interstate auto bridge were no sooner built than they were sold to Union Pacific.*
>
> *In the meantime, work progressed on the grade toward the Sound in 1890, and laborers were paid from $2 to $3 per day. The railroad had a good summer. The railroad charged passengers 50 cents for each run. Lake City became a popular resort, and on many Sundays the cars were full, and people rode on the brake beams. There was a dance hall, a wharf and a boathouse. The Company had placed a steamer, the* Lake City *a 50-passenger boat, and a fleet of sail and rowboats on the lake.*

The road to American Lake, 1889, promoting land sales. Tacoma Illustrated, *Chamber of Commerce.*

In 1892, there were about 100 residents in Lake City. But Hard Times came, with the Panic of 1893, and the Union Pacific went into the hands of Receivers. The railroads continued to operate until 1897 when the rails were taken up. For a decade Lake City ceased to be a suburb of Tacoma. Then Pacific Traction Company built a track from South Tacoma to Lake City and ran electric cars. The place again became a popular resort, with huge crowds on Sundays. There was a privately owned amusement park, with a merry-go-round, swings and a policeman on duty. Lots were again in demand. There were a couple of general stores, a dance hall or two, a laundry at one time, and Martin's Boathouse. The Lake City Church was established in 1922.

The U.S. Government had leased a site on American Lake south for military maneuvers (Camp Murray) for many years. When the land was taken over for Camp Lewis, during WWI many of the farmers moved to Lake City. After the VA Hospital was built in 1922, many of the employees made their homes in the vicinity. Then late in the '30s, things started to boom. Since 1945, the population has gained at a faster rate.

Lake City School District No. 314 was organized in 1892. At first there was one classroom and one teacher. A new school was built in 1914. There were 40 pupils, but it could accommodate 120. The bell was taken to the new school. When the Army took over Camp Lewis, the little town of Hillhurst had to go.

Postcards showing scenes of American Lake, 1909. *Tacoma Public Library, Stenger Collection.*

In 1921, members of the newly organized Community House paid to have a bell hauled from Hillhurst School. The school had been built in 1889, and it was said that the bell came round the Horn. To this day, residents of Lake City are proud of the bell.

Chapter 2

MUMM'S VERY FINE, EXTRA-DRY CHAMPAGNE

The Lake City Land Co. will Offer for Sale on and after May 1, 1889 lots in Their Beautiful Suburban Townsite, Lake City On American Lake. The Tacoma & Lake City Railroad and Navigation Company have placed on the Lake a steamer and a fleet of row and sailboats and have commenced grading the Narrow Gauge Railroad from Tacoma to the Lake. For prices and particulars apply to: Ross & Naubert, 1001 A Street or Smith, Root & Jordan, 919 Pacific Avenue
—Tacoma Daily Ledger, *1889 ad*

Washington Territory officially became a state in 1889, but the Tacoma and Lake City Navigation and Land Company began promoting lots for sale around American Lake six months before statehood was achieved. The Tacoma and Lake City Railroad and Navigation Company built its own railroad line from Twenty-sixth and Union Streets in Tacoma that ran through Oakland, Park Lodge, Flett and Sherwood to Lake City. Its goal was to bring wealthy Tacoma investors to the area. The line terminated at the Lake City Hotel.

LAKEWOOD'S FIRST CITY

In the years between 1880 and 1890, Tacoma's population grew from 1,098 to 36,006. Many newcomers heard of the beautiful lakes south of Tacoma and began coming out in droves.

THE LAKE CITY LAND CO.

Will Offer For Sale

ON AND AFTER MAY 1, 1889,

LOTS IN

Their Beautiful Suburban Townsite,

LAKE CITY

On American Lake.

The Tacoma & Lake City Railroad & Navigation Company have placed on the Lake a steamer and fleet of row and sail boats, and have commenced grading the Narrow Gauge Railroad from Tacoma to the Lake. For prices and particulars apply to

ROSS & NAUBERT,

1001 A Street, or

Smith, Root & Jordan,

919 Pacific Avenue.

A notice about a Lake City Land Co. sale, published in the *Tacoma Daily Ledger*, 1889. *Tacoma Public Library.*

On May 1, 1889, Lake City was declared a city, and that spring, a celebration was held on the shores of American Lake. We can deduce that it was near, if not at, the site of the North American Lake County Park, today renamed as American Lake Park. The Veterans' Hospital was not built until later, and the shores in that direction were often used for tent camping.

The *Tacoma Ledger* tells the story:

> *Carriages, buggies, and other conveyances running the full gamut of the wagon maker's art all decorated in flags and bunting, carried 1,000 persons to American Lake. The procession started decorously enough, but on nearing the city limits it was everyone for himself. Drivers took their choice of a dozen or more trails on the prairie, and some of them galloped their horses to be sure of finding a place to hitch at the lake.*

One of the events at the lake was the launching of the yacht *Lake City*, which went down the waterways with steam up ready to go. Allen C. Mason made a speech from the forward deck, and his small daughter broke a bottle of Mumm's Very Fine, Extra-Dry Champagne over the bow. According to the *Ledger*'s report, the young lady wasn't a good bottle smasher. She broke only the neck at the top, and "as the precious fluid flowed slowly on the deck, Mr. Mason grabbed the bottle and demonstrated a much better use for good champagne."

The railroad declared bankruptcy in 1893 but continued to operate until 1897. By 1907, the Pacific Traction Co. had built a new electric line to Lake City from South Tacoma.

When Camp Lewis was created, many of the displaced farmers moved to Lake City. The 1922 construction of the Veterans' Hospital also attracted new residents.

The real estate office was located in the (Allen C.) Mason Building. Mr. Mason played a role in the promotion of the land sale, as he did in several early Tacoma developments.

The *Tacoma Illustrated* book contains an engraving of all members of the Lake City Navigation Company, including Colonel J.D. Smith and Messrs. Ross, Naubert, F. Campbell, L.T. Root, T.R. Jordan and R.B. Mullen. According to the *Tacoma Illustrated* article, Ross and Naubert were "each the prince of good fellows." Both gentlemen are thoroughly well known in Tacoma.

Mr. Ross landed in the city of Destiny from Pittsfield, Illinois, on December 25, 1879, and had been engaged in the real estate business since 1882. Mr. Naubert, a native of Montreal, Canada, first located in Portland but came

Officers of the Lake City Land Company and the Lake City Railway and Navigation Company, 1889. *Tacoma Chamber of Commerce.*

here in 1881 after he "saw the opportunities that Tacoma offered." For five years, he was cashier of the NP Railroad and left that important position only to engage in his present business (selling real estate).

Charles A. Naubert (left) and Frank C. Ross, agents for Tacoma and Lake City Navigation Company Land Sales, 1889. *Tacoma Public Library.*

> *Besides being owners and dealers in property located in the very best parts of the city, the men, together with other prominent businessmen, have platted and are handling in one of the most picturesque suburban districts of Tacoma: Lake City, a location with enchanting surroundings and bordering on American Lake, the finest sheet of fresh water in Western Washington. This town site will be connected with Tacoma by a railroad that is now nearly completed.*

The men also were connected with the development of the Balfour Dock, the mile-long wharf designed to accommodate oceangoing vessels now known as Tacoma Foss Waterway Seaport.

It is such men as Messrs. Ross and Naubert who have labored so earnestly to bring Tacoma to that destiny that she has attained, namely the metropolis of the Pacific Northwest, and who will be pointed to by future generations as pioneers.

Charles Wright and the Impact of the Tacoma Land Company

Plans for America's transcontinental railroad were in the works as early as the 1850s, when Washington's territorial governor, Isaac Stevens, was charged with finding the best route over the mountains to Puget Sound, but it wasn't until about twenty years later that a decision was made to locate the terminus of the line in the newly established city of Tacoma.

A one-time Pennsylvania oilman, Charles Wright, played a major role in the city's destiny.

Working toward this goal, investors bought up land across the country. Prairies and lakes south of the new city were included in the Tacoma Land Company, and each would play a role in the development of the trains that were on their way.

Not all of Wright's plans went smoothly—in particular, the plans to draw water from American Lake to supply the new city on Commencement Bay.

In the late 1990s, the former power company Puget Sound Power and Light's summer picnic site was sold and converted into a gated residential community known as Eagle Point. It is adjacent to Camp Murray on the south edge of American Lake.

For about twenty years, Steilacoom, established in 1851 and incorporated as the first city in Washington (1854), was the dominant community in the South Puget Sound area. Lafayette Balch, its founder from East Machias, Maine, had grandiose plans for his waterfront town.

When East Coast investors, such as Pennsylvanian Charles Wright, purchased property in Washington Territory and raised money to fund the Northern Pacific Railroad, the focus of development shifted to Tacoma.

Even though Wright did not stay in the Pacific Northwest, he funded the establishment of Annie Wright Seminary, a private girls' school, in the new city to the north, as well as a large city park that bears his name. Years later, in the 1960s, an all-boys' school, Charles Wright Academy, was established near University Place and named for Wright. It has since become co-ed.

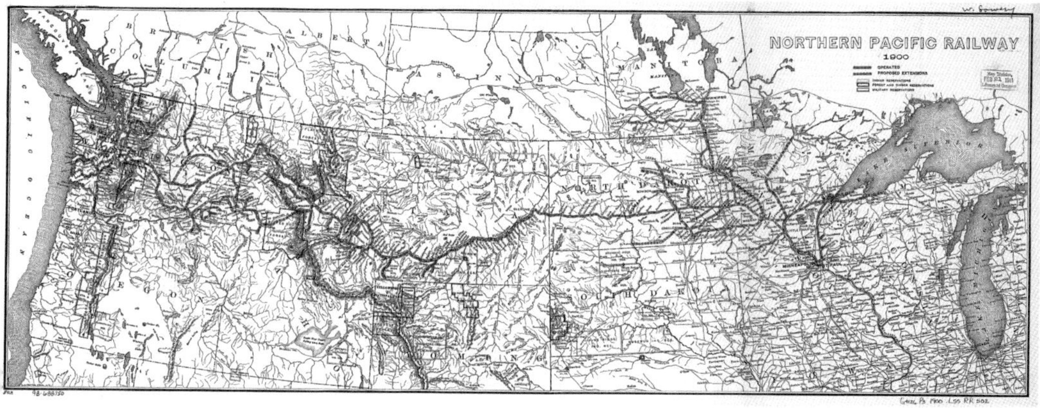

The route of the Great Northern Railway extends across the northern section of the United States to its terminus in Tacoma. On July 2, 1864, Congress chartered the Great Northern Railway Company to link Washington and Oregon to the rest of the country. *Library of Congress.*

Although its holdings are greatly reduced from what they were in 1873, the Tacoma Land Company still exists. Its offices, consisting of three agents and a lead agent, are based on Union Avenue in Tacoma. They primarily oversee recreational properties in eastern Washington, near Brewster and Lake Roosevelt (Silver Spurs Resort, Hawk Creek Resort).

Tacoma Land Company's primary interests in the nineteenth century, however, involved more than making Tacoma the terminus of the Great Northern Railroad (GNR).

The Great Northern Railway map illustration shows the GNR's planned route, which extended across the northern section of the United States to its terminus in Tacoma. On July 2, 1864, Congress chartered the Great Northern Railway Company with the goal of connecting the Great Lakes with the Pacific; opening vast new lands for farming, ranching and mining; and linking Washington and Oregon to the rest of the country. Congress granted 60 million acres of land in exchange for building rail transportation to an undeveloped territory. Some of that land was part of the Tacoma Land Company, with holdings throughout the region, including on American Lake. The first car finally passed through the Puget Sound region on May 27, 1888. In the end, construction of the line took less than 40 million acres.

The Tacoma Land Company, meanwhile, dealt in more than land sales. In 1884, Wright was granted exclusive right to create Tacoma's first power and water company. Water was drawn from Tule and Spanaway Lakes, as well as Clover Creek.

But many Tacomans, especially Tacoma Hotel owner Nelson Bennett, were unhappy about the rates that the company charged for the water, Bennett was especially irate after his hotel's monthly water bill was increased from $75 one month to $502 the following month.

City residents were growing increasingly angry because of an outbreak of typhus since water was brought to the city via a ten-mile wooden flume that emptied into an in-town reservoir. The mostly uncovered flume "attracted thirsty cows, and children in search of a good wading pool."

Editorial cartoonists of the day brandished their poisoned pens and created pointed illustrations. In the December 2, 1892 issue of Randolph Foster Radebaugh's *New West* paper, one artist depicts Theodore Hosmer, brother-in-law of Charles Wright, slouched in a chair at his desk, speaking to "Mr. Chemist," telling him, "I guess we'll take the Spanaway Swamp, Mr. Chemist. Yaas, the bugs are big and the slime is pretty thick, and the taste is a little off, but it's good enough for Tacoma. Then it comes so much cheaper for the 'old man.' The bigger the 'old man's' profits, the bigger my salary is. See?" Mr. Chemist counters: "But here is the pure thing from Maplewood Springs, and the people demand pure water." Hosmer responds, "Oh, that purchase was made just to quiet them."

In his 1916 three-volume *History of Tacoma*, Herbert Hunt writes:

> *Bennett discounted the power company's alleged surveys on Green River. Indeed it was not long before the power company began talking of American Lake as a possible source of supply. That plan was squashed. In a letter that Wright had sent to the council, he said that when he built the Tacoma waterworks, he had expected to live to see the city grow to a population of ten thousand and had planned the system accordingly, but the city had grown to four times that size.*

Eventually, Wright and the city negotiated an agreement wherein Wright sold the light and power plant, worth $600,000, to Tacoma for $1.75 million. Another *New West* cartoon features a monument to Wright along with the caption: "What is a monument to beefsteak?" Tacoma responds, "Not much you don't! All I have left is the purse, and have to hustle up some beefsteak, or die!"

Tacoma Power was created in 1893 when Tacoma's citizens voted to buy the privately owned Tacoma Light and Water Company to ensure its safety and longevity. The first independent power generation came when the LaGrande Dam was constructed on the Nisqually River, thirty-six miles away from Tacoma. Drinking water is piped from the Green River.

Eventually, the City of Tacoma took the water company to court for not fulfilling the terms of its franchise. In 1898, Tacoma, "by order of the court, purchased Tacoma Light and Water Co., thus making Tacoma the first large city in the state to produce its own power."

Despite problems with other aspects of its operation, the Tacoma Land Company proceeded with advertising the land sales development at American Lake.

As a result of the promotions of early realtors such as Allen C. Mason and others, a community on the western shores of American Lake was publicized. In 1889, six months before Washington officially became a state, Lake City was inaugurated with great fanfare—and champagne—on May 1.

Today, Tacoma Public Utilities provides electrical power to Tacoma and the surrounding cities of Fircrest, University Place and Fife; it also provides service to parts of Steilacoom, Lakewood and unincorporated Pierce County. Lakewood Water District, headquartered in Lakewood, today provides water for American Lake's communities. American Lake retains the distinction of having some of the purest waters around.

Allen C. Mason and Company: Promoter of Tacoma's Destiny

Allen C. Mason, an early Tacoma entrepreneur and real estate developer, came west by train in 1883 with his wife, children and in-laws.

One of the first things he did upon his arrival was to rent a shabby center room in a two-story downtown building, where he started his real estate office. (Messrs. Ross and Naubert rented office space from him.) Starting out with very little, he quickly negotiated arrangements with other businessmen and promoted Tacoma through his newspaper ads around the country.

While the Northern Pacific Railroad owned and sold most of the land closest to downtown, Mason focused on outlying neighborhoods. He not only promoted the Point Defiance area, built a gas works business in Olympia and developed an area in Fairhaven (Bellingham), but he also promoted land sales in the American Lake area and personally launched the promotion of Lake City. He and his wife bequeathed to the city their Proctor District library, which first was the location for Whitworth College until 1914 and then became the Weyerhaeuser Mansion.

Bronze statue of Allen C. Mason. Mason was a prominent Tacoma promoter who was involved with the promotion of Lake City at American Lake as an area ripe for development six months before Washington became a state. *Author's collection.*

Among Mr. Mason's well-known local interests, from trolley lines to power plants, was promoting the Lake City Land and Navigation Company, and he personally took part in the project with the May 1, 1889 christening of the steamer *Lake City*.

Like many investors from that era, though, Mason lost his home during the Panic of 1893. In 2008, the Tacoma Historical Society dedicated a bronze statue to Mason in the Proctor District, adjacent to the Anna Lemon Wheelock Branch of the Tacoma Public Library. A burnished Mason, attired in his signature top hat, hand outstretched in greeting, is poised atop a large "star of destiny," representing the star that Mason used in his promotions for the City of Destiny. However, another Tacoman, George Train, is credited with coining the city's "Star of Destiny" motto.

Among his numerous accomplishments, Mason also was renowned for shipping back to Tacoma the 8,500-year-old Egyptian mummy Ankh-Wennefer from Abydos, Egypt, at a cost of $300. In life, according to W.P. Bonney's account, "his mummyship" had been a prophet. After the mummy arrived in the City of Destiny, it was reported that a club comprising unmarried men was formed, taking the mummy's name. The mummy and related artifacts from that expedition were displayed at the Washington State History Museum in 2008. One case contained pieces of Ankh-Wennefer's linen wrappings, which Bonney (at that time curator of the museum) is said to have sold to raise money for the museum.

American Lake Inn

The lake, about ten miles from downtown Tacoma, has been a favorite destination for bicyclists and carriage parties for seventy-five or more years.

The May 20, 1904 *Tacoma Daily Ledger* boasted that "there is no more popular spot in Washington during the summer months than American Lake."

The road from Tacoma to American Lake runs through beautiful, level prairie country dotted with evergreen trees. The only drawback for visitors was lack of suitable hotel accommodations after reaching the lake.

During 1904, a twenty-room summer hotel known as the American Lake Inn formally opened. It was handsomely furnished with a public lobby, a ladies' parlor, a private dining room and a main dining room with accommodations for sixty people.

Illustration of American Lake Inn, a twenty-room resort at Lake City, American Lake, circa 1904. *Tacoma Public Library.*

In addition, a handsome pavilion had also been built on the lakeshore for the use of guests. There also was a boathouse and bathhouse open to the public every day. The rate to regular boarders was ten dollars per week; children under ten years were charged five dollars per week. Single meals were fifty cents. During July of that summer, a steam launch on the lake could be chartered for special parties or trips around the lake.

A front-page item in the September 16, 1929 issue of the *Tacoma Daily Ledger* reported that a fire had destroyed the old hotel at American Lake. An early assessment valued the loss at $5,000:

> *The structure was empty at the time, without furniture, with the exception of personal belongings owned by five men who had set up bachelor quarters. Firemen from nearby Ft. Lewis responded, but the building was too far gone to be saved.*
>
> *Mrs. Thomas Clay, who resides near the hotel, had purchased the hotel, but she could not be reached, and it was not known whether the loss was covered by insurance.*
>
> *State Highway Patrolman H.O. Snyder took charge of the crowd and restored order in a short time.*

On August 27, 1912, according to the *News Tribune*'s "Looking Back" section, prizes for the Labor Day Celebration at American Lake included everything from a side of bacon to a box of hole-proof socks. Besides that, the biggest prizes would be awarded in the fifty-yard race for married couples. First prize was a $10.00 dinner set; second, a $4.00 rocker; and third, $3.50 in trade at a furniture store.

In 2012, Lake City was reported to have a population of 15,729 in an area that measured 8.496 square miles (as determined by the City of Lakewood) and stretched from the lakeshore to Steilacoom Boulevard—far larger than the original city site.

Neighboring Tillicum (a Chinook word that translates as "friend" or "friendly village"), meanwhile, in 2000 had a population of 2,037 in a 0.49-square-mile area.

In 2013, Lake City and Tillicum were regarded as "neighborhoods" of Lakewood; their council representatives were Paul Bocchi and John Simpson. Monthly neighborhood association meetings were held in both communities. Of the two today, Tillicum's neighborhood association is more active.

Lake City, a small strip of land that began its existence in 1889 with high hopes of one day becoming a full-fledged city, today has a more established appearance than other Lakewood neighborhoods. It is the setting for a church; a Veterans' Administration Hospital; an elementary school; a city park; assorted businesses, including a daycare facility; boat

View of American Lake Park, where Tacoma Land and Navigation Co. held its launch of the *Lake City* steamboat, 1889. *Author's collection.*

repair; several convenience stores and taverns; a small fast-food restaurant; a laundromat; and a dentist and is filled with many memories about living in Tacoma's Playground.

Tillicum is a narrow strip of land on the eastern side of the lake that encompasses primarily a commercial strip focusing on its predominantly military clientele, a library, a boathouse, assorted housing, two gated communities and a large city park.

Albert Abner Silcox Buys and Names His Island

One of the earliest twentieth-century property owners on American Lake was A.A. Silcox, who purchased a thirteen-acre island close to the lake's western shore.

In a document dated June 10, 1898, Mr. C. O'Brian of the Tacoma Land Company wrote the following to J.W. Anderson:

> *Dear Sir,*
> *Abner Silcox has completed the clearing of lands and shrubs at American Lake. The total area of land cleared is forty-four (44) acres, which at $40 per acre, amounts to nineteen hundred and eighty (1,980) dollars. The above amount—less the amount of payments made—is now due him.*
> *Respectfully submitted*

A footnote explains, "While Albert Abner Silcox was fulfilling his contract with the Tacoma Land Company for clearing land in 1893, he lived with his family in a cabin on the estate of S.N. Nolan on American Lake." The Nolan house was a large four-story showplace called Bell Mar Villa, and Nolan was one of the members of the Tacoma Land Company. Bell Mar Villa was built in 1880 but demolished in 1917, when the United States government bought the property for its new military camp, known as Fort Lewis. The piece of property was used later in 1923 as the site for the American Lake Veterans' Administration Hospital.

A stained-glass window from Nolan's Bell Mar Villa was later incorporated into one of the small "shacks" that A.A. built.

According to a note in the *History of Lakewood* by Lakewood historians/authors Walter Neary and Steve Dunkelberger, Stephen Nolan later sold his property to the Visitation Sisters, who in turn sold it and built Visitation

Mrs. Nolan's Cottage near American Lake. Illustration from the Pacific Traction Company's newsletter, *The Forum*, 1904. *Tacoma Public Library.*

Villa on a one-hundred-acre piece of property in Lakewood. From 1924 to 1957, the Visitation School for Girls operated there until the property was sold again and Lakewood's second shopping center, Villa Plaza, was built on the site.

The island that Silcox purchased is the one featured in the 1889 *Tacoma Daily Ledger* article about the launch of the steamboat *Lake City*, operating on the lake to show prospective property owners the land that was available for future home sites.

In the late 1800s, when the Tacoma Land Company (TLC) announced the sale of property around American Lake, Albert Abner Silcox decided he wanted to live there. In 1893, he agreed to work for the TLC, clearing property at the south end of the lake to earn money to pay for his piece of this glacier-created chunk of paradise.

During that time, Silcox and his family lived in a cabin on the estate of Stephen W. Nolan. Nolan, a turn-of-the-century land baron, owned Tacoma Carriage and Transfer.

For clearing forty-five acres of land that eventually became part of the Veterans' Administration Hospital in 1923, Mr. Silcox earned $1,980—at the rate of $40 per acre. A portion of that money—$350—was used to pay for his thirteen-acre island.

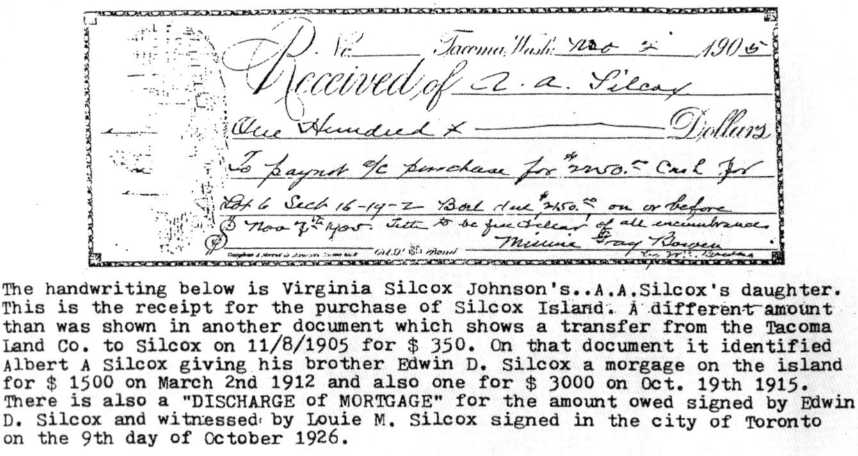

No. ___ Tacoma, Wash. Nov 4 1905

Received of A. A. Silcox

One Hundred x ——— Dollars

To payment o/c purchase for $250.00 Cash for

Lot 6 Sect 16-19-2 Bal due $250.00 on or before

Nov 7th 1905. Title to be free & clear of all encumbrance.

Minnie Gray Bowen

The handwriting below is Virginia Silcox Johnson's..A.A.Silcox's daughter. This is the receipt for the purchase of Silcox Island. A different amount than was shown in another document which shows a transfer from the Tacoma Land Co. to Silcox on 11/8/1905 for $ 350. On that document it identified Albert A Silcox giving his brother Edwin D. Silcox a morgage on the island for $ 1500 on March 2nd 1912 and also one for $ 3000 on Oct. 19th 1915. There is also a "DISCHARGE of MORTGAGE" for the amount owed signed by Edwin D. Silcox and witnessed by Louie M. Silcox signed in the city of Toronto on the 9th day of October 1926.

Copy of a receipt for payment on Silcox Island. *Courtesy of Susan Gierke collection.*

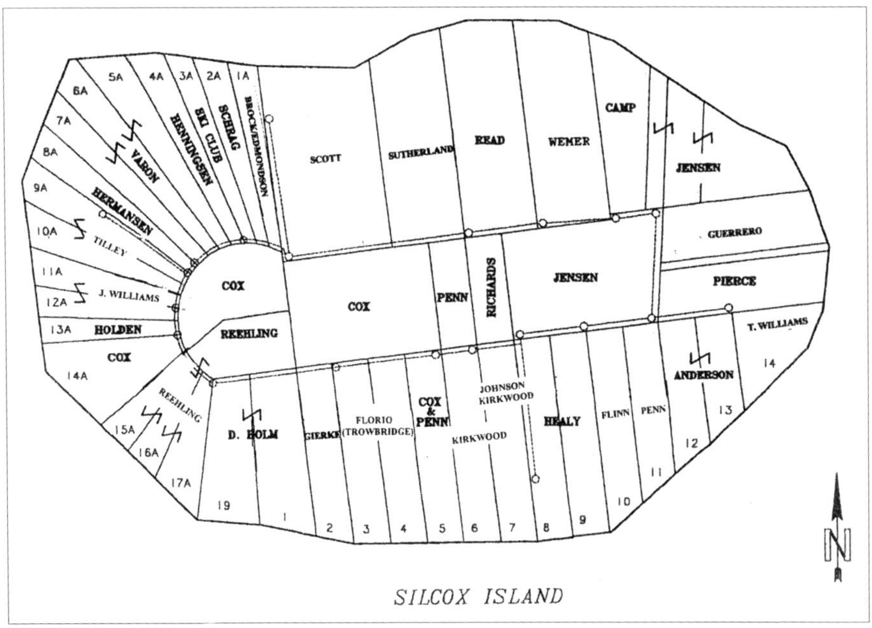

Map illustration of Silcox Island properties. *Courtesy of Susan Gierke collection.*

According to the family history, Silcox immigrated to the United States from Ontario with his wife, Betsy; four daughters; and a son. After their only son died unexpectedly in 1902 at the end of a close basketball game between old Tacoma High and Everett High, Silcox was devastated. Hard work kept his sorrow at bay, and three years later, he made the payment on his island on the lake, where he moved his family; built his home, known as the "Big House"; and began construction on a hodgepodge assortment of small cabins. Today, there are twenty-six properties around the island.

Silcox published an ad in 1911 advising potential renters to ask for A.A. Silcox at the old house "where the flag is flying."

With its proximity to Camp Murray and Fort Lewis, according to the Silcox Island family history book, sometimes soldiers (and their lady friends) rowed to the island for some "snuggling." Silcox usually chased them off, reminding them that the island was private property. Other times, feeling a bit mischievous, he'd untie the soldier's boat and push it adrift on the lake. When a sheepish-looking soldier knocked at the door of the Big House, Silcox would row the couple back to the shore, lecturing them soundly during the crossing about their improprieties.

In 2005, Silcox Islanders celebrated a centennial by collecting photos and memories of their century on Albert A.'s land. While a few residents live there year round, for the majority of the residents, the island is their personal summer camp.

View of Silcox Island from Harry Todd Park. Mr. Silcox purchased the thirteen-acre island for $350 in 1904. *Author's collection.*

Dorothy Johnson Holm (Virginia Silcox Johnson's daughter) wrote that the island was first their summer home:

> *At first, we had to go by train to Camp Murray, walk down to the lake laden with eats, etc. We had our boat parked where Murray Creek ran into the lake. We couldn't park a horse and buggy (with the fringe on top) on the lake for two days. We already had a home there that had been built by an Englishman* [whose name she could not remember, but she said that it was called the "Big House," which was inherited by Bess Reehling and later given to Joyce (now Mrs. Sid Cox)].
>
> *Later we had a big garden, fruit trees, and we girls had to pack water from the pump back of the house to the garden. How well I remember that job! We also had chickens that summer, and dad also floated a cow across, so we lived "high on the hog" so to speak.*
>
> *Later an electric car* [trolley] *ran from Town to Tillicum, which made it easier for us as we never had an automobile. There were four girls: Virginia, Fannie (who died in 1936); Bess, (now living in Seattle) and Bertha, who passed away after marriage, Her husband was Mitchell Southerland, who for many years was automobile editor for the* Seattle Times.

Silcox Island's 2005 centennial book is filled with recollections of summers spent on A.A.'s island:

> *Grandpa Bert was thin, over six feet, with white hair and always wore a black suit with white shirt and suspenders. When we went to the mainland, I was allowed to stand on a chair and brush his hair and suit. I begged to row, and at five years of age, he finally let me. He never had to row again! Smart man!*

About her father, Ed Johnson, Dorothy wrote: "Dad took an extra job after we moved in [on the island], by bartending at the BBQ Inn on Saturday nights. He couldn't drink liquor as it made him deathly sick, but he learned how to mix drinks, and everyone was his friend!"

Virginia Silcox, Albert's eldest daughter, remembered coming to the island as a young girl, taking the train to Camp Murray, where the Silcoxes kept their boat pulled up in the bushes. Later, when the streetcars ran to Tillicum, they pulled their boat up and stored it in the bushes nearby.

Until the mid-1960s, when electricity came to the island, all the work on the island was done manually—the women's husbands improvised on all their construction projects.

Albert Silcox was a very ambitious man. Between 1899 and 1924, he operated a furniture store in Tacoma.

Susan Holm Gierke's (Albert's great-granddaughter) ambition is to someday write a book about her Silcox Island memories called *Great-Grandfather's Gift.*

In 1997, *News Tribune* writer Bart Ripp wrote a feature about the "tranquil retreat in American Lake," in which he summarized Silcox Island's history. Susan's parents, Dorothy and Clary Holm, compiled a home-style history about the island. Photocopies of Holm's papers make for interesting reading in the Tacoma Public Library's Northwest Room.

Pacific Traction: A New Factor for Tacoma

"Before 1907 becomes very old," according to *The Forum*, the Pacific Traction Company's 1906 broadsheet, "PTC was to have in operation full cars and more than 20 miles of rails that were to be laid in the city. In addition to this [the boom days of railroad development] the American Lake line will be in operation, and probably taxing the cars to capacity."

The Forum featured photos showing the Nolan's "cottage," Bell Mar Villa and the American Lake Inn, with twenty rooms and a view of "beautiful American Lake" on the Pacific Traction Company's Line.

The publication further boasted that

> *quick transit means the building of more homes. If the workingman's car trip is shortened a few moments each day, the time he saves in a few years is no small item. The Traction Company will spend $1 million in its present work when it is complete, believing that Tacoma now has a population of 86,000, and recognizing the friendly feeling existing between the company and its prospective patrons, the investment of the Traction Company looks like a grass root proposition.*

Sound Transit's twenty-first-century mass transportation system has its roots in Tacoma's trolley system of the 1880s. Horse-drawn trolleys replaced the original steam-driven cars, and after just a year, electric cars replaced the horses. The train company was the world's first interurban streetcar system. It was at that time the longest electric line in the world (twelve miles).

Besides the route between Steilacoom and Tacoma, other passenger trolley companies were developed. Their tracks shuttled residents around Tacoma and the outlying areas. American Traction Line went to Manitou and Lake City. By 1928, only three companies remained: Pacific Traction, which ran tracks to American Lake; the Tacoma Railway and Power Company, which operated to Steilacoom; and the Puget Sound Electric Railway, which ran lines to Kent and Seattle.

Although the lines were discontinued in the 1930s, by 1999, Tacoma voters approved a tax to establish another light rail line (Tacoma Link). It began operating in 2003. Tacoma City Council approved plans in 2013 to extend the line from Pacific Avenue to the Hilltop area and begin charging for its usage.

Chapter 3

BUILDING AROUND THE LAKE

East and West Sides

Chester Thorne

Among the early Tacoma "movers and shakers" who bought property from the Tacoma Land Company was Chester L. Thorne.

Chester served as chairman of the board of directors of the National Bank of Tacoma, was a member of the Port of Tacoma's board and was instrumental in the establishment of Paradise at Mount Rainier and in promoting the sale of property south of American Lake to the U.S. government, which became Joint Base Lewis-McChord.

Born on November 11, 1863, Chester was the son of Edwin Thorne of New York and grandson of Jonathan Thorne of England, whose ancestors came to America before the Revolutionary War. Chester's brother, Oakleigh, owned the family property in New York.

Thorne attended Yale, graduated in 1884 with a bachelor of philosophy degree in engineering and was hired in the Engineering Department at Missouri Pacific Railway in St. Louis.

After completing his training in real estate, he married Anna Hoxie of Des Moines, Iowa, in 1890. The Thornes were parents of four children, three of whom died early. Anita, born in 1895, was the sole surviving child. Chester settled in the Tacoma area and became a director of the Bank of Commerce.

In 1911, Thorne's American Lake home, Thornewood Castle, was built. Thorne's authentic "castle" on the shore of American Lake in Lakewood,

Thornewood Castle, Tillicum, built in 1911. *Tacoma Public Library.*

Washington (Tillicum), is one of the truly private castles in the country. Renowned nineteenth-century architect Kirtland Cutter designed it. The lavish home contains crystal windows made in England, along with stained-glass panels dating from as early as AD 1300 that were transported to American Lake.

The structure contains fifty-four rooms, of which twenty-eight are bedrooms and twenty-two are baths, and allegedly, according to one website, there are a few resident ghosts that float around—understandable since the castle's building materials were recycled from authentic English structures.

Thorne, a Port of Tacoma founder, had this three-story twenty-seven-thousand-square-foot mansion built in the early twentieth century. Only the very best of materials, including four-hundred-year-old bricks from an original English castle, were used. Thorne's ornate home was built to last for centuries, a plan Thorne ensured through the use of a three-foot-thick foundation, eighteen-inch floors of concrete, ten-inch cinderblock walls and hand-hewn woodwork from ancient English oak, held together by solid wood dowels. In order to transport the original bricks, Thorne commissioned three ships to transport the materials around Cape Horn to the Pacific Northwest.

Thornewood Gardens. After the house was built, Thorne commissioned a landscape architect to turn thirty-seven of the estate's one hundred acres into formal English gardens. It required twenty-eight full-time gardeners to tend the grounds, while another full-time staff of forty servants tended to the needs of Thorne and his family. *Library of Congress.*

After the house was built, Thorne commissioned a landscape architect to turn thirty-seven acres of the estate's one hundred acres into formal English gardens. It required twenty-eight full-time gardeners to tend the grounds, while another full-time staff of forty servants tended to the needs of Thorne; his wife, Anna; and their daughter, Anita. At that time, Thornewood's gardens were considered to be the finest gardens in the country.

The Thornes' daughter, Anita, married Cadwallader Corse and, along with the Corses' son and daughter, continued to live at the castle until they divorced. During the Thornes' tenure, the couple hosted numerous summer "white" teas, at which guests were encouraged to dress in white.

Mr. Thorne was very private about his business dealings. There were many whom he backed with loans—helping them to get on their feet, steadying them and starting them anew.

Thornewood Castle gardens, 1923. *Library of Congress.*

Daily Ledger editor Herbert Hunt wrote about Thorne, "There is no finer work in life than this."

During the Panic of 1893, it's reported that Thorne did not have to close his bank.

Chester, who died in 1927, enjoyed his castle for only about a decade, but his wife, Anna, was elected to fill the vacancy on the board of directors of her husband's bank and continued to oversee her late husband's philanthropic efforts in the community.

Three weeks after Chester Thorne's death, a news article reported that another tragedy had struck Thornewood. Two ambulances were sent to the estate, but all that's known is that one of them left carrying an injured Cadwallader. Newspapers reported that he had suffered an accident when a rifle he was carrying went off, lodging a bullet in his head. The next day, his right eyeball was removed, along with the bullet behind it. The true circumstances of this episode have never been publicly explained.

After her divorce from Corse, in 1936 Anita married Captain David Stone, the former Fort Lewis quartermaster, who oversaw construction of the 1917 fort and later was promoted to major general. While her husband was stationed in Panama, Chester's widow, Anna, lived in a smaller home that she had built in North Tacoma. Anna returned to Thornewood after her daughter and husband returned to Washington. She died peacefully in 1954.

Rose Red Haunts American Lake

While Chester Thorne and his castle were well known to early area residents, today his fifty-four-room abode is probably better known as the filming location for a television adaptation of horror author Stephen King's *Rose Red*.

In 2000, Thornewood's current owners, Deanna and Wayne Robinson, arranged with Disney-ABC to use this lavish lakeside mansion as the ideal setting for King's gothic horror story about a spirit-possessed mansion.

During the course of the horror tale's filming, the mansion was restored to its original condition. One evening, its guests enjoyed a special premiere of the made-for-TV series.

Although many residents in the area were unaware of the house's history, once the filming was completed, the castle, for a time, became the popular setting for formal tea parties.

The castle is now used as a bed-and-breakfast, as well as the setting for weddings, anniversaries and other milestone events.

One recent special event, the fourth season finale for the popular HBO series *Game of Thrones*, was held at the castle on June 15, 2014. Approximately 160 *Game of Thrones* fans attended the festivities, many attired in *Game of Thrones* attire.

Renowned Architect Left His Mark on American Lake and Fort Lewis

Spokane's famous Davenport Hotel, the *Spokane Chronicle* building and even a modest home in Metaline Falls that has been used as a community theater are just a few examples of the many early twentieth-century buildings designed by an Ohioan who came west to follow his career.

Once Kirtland Cutter began his practice in Spokane in the late nineteenth century, he branched out to designing homes in this area for about thirty years. He concluded his career in 1939 in California.

One of Cutter's most distinctive local works, the Fort Lewis entrance gates, is visible to motorists traveling on the main route of I-5. The gateway to the military establishment, built of rough-hewn stone and logs, took its inspiration from the design of forts in the early years of Washington Territory. Two "fortified" blockhouses, similar to those that existed at Fort Nisqually, near Tacoma, supported a canopy made of whole tree trunks spanning the roadway. Some arches allowed the passage of pedestrians on either side.

Chester Thorne was instrumental in having the military camp located on the site near American Lake and "may have helped secure the gateway commission for Cutter."

Ambrose Russell Designs Lake City Elementary School

Structure Well Equipped and Modern—Good Program Given

Two hundred patrons of the Lake City School District at American Lake gathered on October 13, 1916 at the dedication ceremonies of their new school building and escorted visitors through the splendid modern structure. They are truly proud of the new home of knowledge, for it is one of the finest country schools on the Pacific Coast, comprising as it does an auditorium, gymnasium, shower baths, manual training and domestic science departments. Tacoma architect Ambrose Russell designed this structure; it was the only school he designed. Its distinctive cupola still soars above that 1916 structure.

The lighting arrangement is perfect and by night, gas is used as an illuminant. The auditorium, especially constructed for neighborhood gathering and amateur performances, was well filled last night.

The board of directors of the district is made up of W.E. Morris chairman; Alice B. Woodroofe and Andrew Lowe. Mr. Morris was the chairman of the dedicatory exercises. Cost of the structure? $13,000.

Springtime view of Lake City Elementary Cupola. Lake City's Elementary School was designed in 1916 by renowned Tacoma architect Ambrose Russell. *Author's collection.*

Christened with National Hymn

The audience sang "America" with gusto and baptized the new schoolhouse with the national hymn. Mr. Morris welcomed the visitors and introduced the speakers.

Miss Fern Jones, teacher of the younger pupils, teaches them something additional to the three R's, for a number of them did a shoemaker's dance. The intricate movements were performed and the youngsters went about their work with a keen zest. W.C. Bertram of Tacoma sang a Scotch song and Miss Jessie Lowe danced a Highland dance, the Seann Triubbas, and her father demonstrated that he is capable of being musical as well as directing the affairs of the district. He played the pipes as an accompaniment, giving a true Caledonian tang to the number.

E.E. Crook, assistant superintendent of the Tacoma schools, congratulated the residents of the district on their enterprise in providing such an institution for the betterment of their children.

Judge Fremont Campbell contrasted educational advantages in that locality now to a quarter of a century ago, when he was raising his family there. "The boys and the girls of today are brighter than they were in that day, and they ought to be, for they have superior facilities for gaining knowledge. This is a school of today and expresses the ideals of the present."

Miss Isabel Pratt is principal of the school and her students sang a spring song under her direction and with her accompaniment.

Should Develop Citizenship

"We may bring forth everything Washington can produce, but if we do not bring forth citizens who can master these valleys and conquer the mountains, we have failed," said Dr. E.H. Todd, president of the College of Puget Sound, when called upon for an extemporaneous address. "Character building is what this school is for, and I think that the training of men to be trusted is all important.

"Creation of ideals is what we want. Some time in the past some man saw this school building in his brain. Then he carried the message to others, and finally we see the reality. But that man had to have the ideal before this structure could be. We must teach the child to think and then we have ideals. Let us offer a silent prayer that God will be with you in your work every day."

J.B. Mitchell spoke about manual training in the schools, and L.L. Benbow gave words of encouragement to the directors. Misses Margaret Russell, Florence Coates and Dorothy James did the graceful Highland fling, and it was done so well it fairly breathed of the land of the heather. Again Mr. Lowe played the war pipes. The audience closed the exercises with the singing of the "Star Spangled Banner."

The building was erected at a cost of $13,000 and is forty by seventy feet in size. The auditorium on the top floor occupies the entire floor space of the building and carries out the idea of using the schoolhouse of today for something else besides mere textbook instruction. A metal port cochere is to be erected over each of the doors. Actual work will begin Monday on the two rooms, which will have accommodations for sixty students, the present enrollment, and 150 children may be taught when the occasion requires.

Lake City School Modernization and Rededication

On November 18, 1975, at least 350 former Lake City Elementary School students, parents and residents of the Lake City community gathered at the "little red schoolhouse" to rededicate the remodeled 1916 structure.

Suburban Times reporter Terry Campbell chronicled highlights of the celebration with assorted visitors' comments: "We had a real snappy girls' basketball team," "This used to be the gym," "I'm very proud of the school."

The cost of the remodel was $137,000, and the building, originally constructed in 1916 for $13,000, was predicted to serve as an educational facility for another sixty-three years.

Among those at the rededication was Janette (Holt) Lee, who first came to Lake City as a four-and-a-half-year-old. She attended classes in the original building and later served as a cook at the school.

When she was a student there, a five-minute bell signaled the start of classes for the day. Pupils lined up and entered into the building to the sounds of a Sousa march.

Snippets of those long-ago schoolday recollections included music, art and government, with domestic science for fourth- and fifth-grade girls and manual training for boys. School assemblies for special holidays, lots of plays and even operettas were staged in the auditorium.

Sign for Harrison Preparatory School, Lake City (contemporary home to Harrison Preparatory School). *Author's collection.*

One year, in preparation for the annual September Puyallup Fair, hundreds of tissue paper mums were created for a fair display.

Gymnastics were held every day, and if the weather was bad, the students ran up and down the aisles. Lake City was strong in sports, with track meets as major yearly events.

Katherine (Williams) Andrews, who attended the school from 1909 to 1917 recalled that the school year ended with a special program that included speeches and recitations and concluded with a picnic at American Lake.

Tacoma News Tribune building writer Carl Lizberg reported that when the 1916 structure was built, it was the only school in the Lakes School District. When a previous structure burned to the ground, the little red schoolhouse promptly took its place. He wrote:

> *Now it struggles to keep its high gabled roof and bell tower visible to passersby from the more modern school built in recent years. The historic structure has 20 sister schools in the Clover Park District, which absorbed the Lake City School in 1941.*

A view of the original Lake City Elementary School, Lake City. *Author's collection.*

> *The building's fate was studied for many years, even as its classrooms continued to be used, despite the deterioration which continued. Then in 1974 plans were made to remodel the building. Tacoma architects Rue and Butler were hired for the project, with Saule Construction of Lakewood and Allan V. Creten, engineer.*
>
> *The building now houses a new Instructional Materials Center* [library] *and a Group Instruction Space for team teaching.*

At the time when this Lake City/Tillicum book project was begun, the classes constituting Lake City Elementary's Harrison Prep School were scheduled to be relocated to Clover Park Technical College. The future of the Lake City Elementary School building had not yet been determined. The preparatory classes, begun at that school about ten years earlier, were being moved to the campus of Clover Park Technical College—once the site of the Tacoma Speedway—with plans to enroll eight hundred students to the new site in the winter of 2015.

Lake City's Community Clubhouse

A project that began thirty-eight years ago with an old schoolhouse that was moved to the present site reached a climax when the neighboring Lake City Community Club held its open house on the shores of American Lake.

Lake City Community Club. *Author's collection.*

The new Lake City Community clubhouse was virtually complete and had actually been in use for nearly a year as a meeting place for members, Girl Scouts, Sunday school and dancing lessons.

The Lake City Lutheran parish had also been using the building for services while its church was under construction near the Idlewild School.

The new clubhouse was built entirely with volunteer labor and was debt free, according to club president Robert DeSilva.

That program featured entertainment and refreshments, introduction of past presidents and family members of the club's founders.

The Lake City Community Club began in 1920, when residents subscribed funds to purchase land and pay a contractor to move the old Lake City school building to the present site, which was then the property of the Clover Park School District. Since that time, the old school has been used as a community center by Lake City residents.

According to early notes about Lake City Community Club, it was organized by local people as an open club with all meetings open to the public. The club purchased the present building—an old school that was demolished in the early '60s and rebuilt—for one dollar. Through all the club's ups and downs, dues have stayed at one dollar per family per year, despite inflation. Through the years, the club has served as a meeting place for Girl Scouts, Brownies, Cub Scouts, Boy Scouts and teenage groups and as a polling place.

The club's role was to provide a meeting place for events that fostered community spirit. It was incorporated to maintain a social center for affairs tending toward the social and moral uplifting of the community. That original property was sold to the school district, after which the club began construction of the new clubhouse.

The new clubhouse reflected the growth that came to the community after World War II.

The community itself was first settled in the 1850s and platted in 1889 under its present name. Since its beginnings, the resort community has had its challenges as a place that drew large crowds of people from Tacoma seeking amusement and relaxation.

> *The community's steady growth in population was connected to the establishment of Fort Lewis and the Veterans Hospital that was built in 1922. Military personnel and civilians for both installations have played a considerable role in the growth of Lake City and its community club…*

An article in the August 7, 1960 *News Tribune* said that the

> *fifty by eighty foot building was expected to be completed by early fall. Cost of construction was $2,500—or little more than fifty cents per square foot. Another $1,000 should handle heat and lighting. Other towns may be amazed at the minimum of expense and the enthusiasm of the teenagers whose devotion and industry set a wholesome example.*

The building of the gymnasium was a great effort by primarily the teenage kids of Lake City in the summer of 1960. They became interested in what they were building for themselves and gave up most of their vacations so they could get the job done. The professional builders in the neighborhood, such as the McKasson brothers, Earl Keehn and Ray Lueger, were very helpful. Their time was all donated, as was that of the many parents who stopped by.

Among the club's achievements was improvement of the county dock at Lake City Boulevard. Club members were instrumental in getting American Lake North Park going and did much of the labor and ground work for the park. They also were instrumental in getting Lake City District zoned.

Club officers included Alvin Stearns, president; Rose Parkinson, secretary; Carsten Peterson, treasurer; Griff Perlman, director; Earl

Keehn, director; and Les Linbo, director. Parkinson was the club's secretary from 1957 to 1958.

(In 2012, the clubhouse closed, and its future was yet to be determined.)

Liz Parkinson Remembers

Liz Parkinson, whose photo is featured in a 1961 *News Tribune* story about the community club, shared her recollections of the club. "My parents, Rose and Jim Parkinson, came from South Dakota," she said. Liz's father had a promising career with Bell Telephone, which abruptly ended with the stock market crash of 1929. He went through a tough time, married Rose in 1937 and came west. He worked in the dining room at Western State Hospital; Rose later joined him. The first night she was here, she was amazed to see every patient having strawberries for dessert. (At that time, the hospital raised its own food.) Rose never forgot that image, nor the wonderful things she discovered in the Northwest. She loved the mountains and the water. She loved the green and gardened with a passion.

Liz was born in 1944. By 1953, she had finished third grade at Visitation Catholic School in South Tacoma. Her parents paid $4,500 for their Newgrove Avenue home. The property was just shy of an acre, and at one time it included a barn and horses. It also had its own well (which was later filled in), and there was a "sunken garden" with bleeding hearts and primroses. Liz said she felt as though she'd been transported to her own Secret Garden. There also were rambling roses. Liz believed they were grown from historic cuttings, and they bloom along the fence every summer.

The Parkinson house was located one block east of Veteran's Drive. After Liz's parents settled into the house, doing a lot of painting, remodeling and gardening, they began meeting other people in the community. It was a time when people were interested in the community, and everyone wanted to contribute something. Rose decided to write the history of Lake City.

Her history was based on information that she found in the archives at the Washington State Historical Society (now the Ferry Museum, next to Stadium High School). She determined to research the history independently, finding resources where she could.

"Imagine not having the Internet," said Liz.

Rose assembled her research and presented it at a community club meeting. Liz recalled that Rose was "very nervous" because she was not accustomed to public speaking.

View of American Lake from American Lake Park. *Author's collection.*

Some things that Liz remembered:

The house where the Parkinsons lived was originally two cabins, joined with a common kitchen area. The families came to the lake via trolley or train and stayed for the summer.

There was a park; a hotel; "maybe a dance pavilion," Liz thought; and rowboats to rent.

Lake City was pretty much designated as a resort area, with a public beach, at the present Pierce County Park (now American Lake Park) and another public access at the end of Naomilawn Avenue. Later, there was a seaplane park. There also was a link to Tillicum Beach and Park and Silcox Island.

There were two markets or general stores until the '60s: Rowan's and Holt's. At Rowan's there was a meat market with a full-time butcher who wrapped the meat in white paper, and it "was all so fresh."

American Lake was absolutely beautiful (and still is), fed by springs that kept the water crystal clear, with Mount Rainier and its snow-draped slopes in the background at the north end.

Brunson's Market—on the edge of the Lake City community, along Washington Boulevard—is located at the site of Peugh's Corner. Liz's dad got his haircuts from "Old Man Peugh." Liz said that she often sat and waited for her dad and always wondered about the history of the place.

Lakeside Country Club

Near the southern corner of Veteran's Drive (closest to Gravelly Lake Drive) is a walled community that's marked by a heavenly looking wrought-iron gate. An engraved brass plaque on the wall announces that the place is the Lakeside Country Club (LCC)—small by most country club standards—but that wasn't always true.

While Tacoma's oldest country club, the Tacoma Country and Golf Course (TC&GC, established in 1894), is located kitty-corner across American Lake from LCC, Lake City's sole country club is nevertheless the "oldest" in that lakeside community.

Young bachelor businessmen from Tacoma came to the area shortly after the Tacoma Land Company began promoting the lake area for potential home sites. By 1910, sixty-one members had signed a letter of incorporation. Those signing the club's "Articles of Incorporation" included F.B. Crocker, David Rickden, P. Rorry, F.F. Lawrence, Carl V. Ross. W.L. Bair, August Van Boecklin and E.L. Aldrich.

Those early members came to the lake area during the summer months, first bringing rough camping equipment. Next, they built small cabins and eventually purchased the property and began building homes on the acreage.

Gated entryway to Lakeside Country Club, located along Veteran's Drive. *Author's collection.*

Over time, those original members expanded the site and developed a nine-hole golf course across from the housing area. After the Veterans' Hospital was built in the early 1920s, the golf course property was sold. Today, the former LCC golf course site is occupied by Stanley Estates—a "mature adult" housing complex of thirty units—as well as other single-family homes.

Like the TC&GC at the north end of the lake, Lakeside also has had two former clubhouses, both of which were lost to fires. The current clubhouse, like the previous ones, serves as a location for other social events such as birthdays, anniversaries and other celebrations.

A single narrow path winds its way from that imposing front entrance gate toward the lake and beach on the southwest corner of American Lake. The "club" encompasses nineteen houses in this gated lakeside community; all have evolved from the original cabins built there in the early 1900s.

According to current resident/club member/historian Sharon Montgomery, who, along with her husband, Clark, resides in one of the oldest houses (1908) on the site, it began in 1904 as a bachelors' canoe club. A windmill on the Ambrose Russell property originally provided water for club residents. An informal tour through the Montgomerys' home reveals a lot of tiny rooms, cubbyholes in size—just real old-fashioned charm. Many of the existing homes in Lakeside, Sharon says, had their beginnings as summer cabins built by members of the Canoe Club who eventually formed the country club.

Those early 1900s canoe trips evolved into camping trips with small canvas tents. They, in turn, evolved into cabins and eventually into houses.

In 1946, Dick Perkins, whose family resided at number 17 and purchased the lot from Joseph Baker in 1940, wrote the following account in 1946 for his third period "Northwest History" class at Clover Park High School:

> *The* [h]*istory of the Lakeside Club, as far back as its history goes (1904), we find that at first a bunch of bachelors organized a club in Tacoma, bought some land and lake frontage on North American Lake, erected a clubhouse, hired a caretaker (the first of these is said by many sources to have been Joseph and Mary Holt, who now own a thriving concession in Lake City) and came on weekends for their meals and threw many a gay party. Mr. Holt is credited with building the Holt Chapel, which eventually was expanded into the Lake City Community Church.*
>
> *In fact, many of the first club members came out because of these parties. Then some of these bachelors married, brought their families out here and lived in tent houses. Of course, then there were no sidewalks; few, if any lights, no lights in houses, no lawns and, last of all, no watering system.*

> *The ladies and men then hauled the water from the lake, boiled it and then used it. Later a water tower was erected.*

On June 17, 1908, club resident Howard E. Gregory wrote the following entry in his diary:

> *There is one large island and about seven small ones in the lake. The large one was, quite recently, owned by Mr. Silcox and lies opposite our camp, nearer the eastern shore of the lake. There are three summer residences on this island…*
>
> *One thing in particular I noticed concerning the islands, and that is that pine trees grow in no other part near the lake, except on the islands. The trees of the islands are not large enough on Silcox Island, where they grow to the same size as those on the shore of the lake.*
>
> *American Lake may be reached from Tacoma by the Northern Pacific, Tacoma Railroad and Power Company, or the Pacific Traction Company lines. The first two run along the eastern bank of the lake, while the Pacific Traction line runs along the western bank. The T.R. and P line terminates nearly opposite our camp at American Lake, and the Pac. Trac. Line terminates about a mile northwest of our camp at Traction Park, near Lake City.*

Lakeside Country Club tennis court decorated for the centennial. The club is Lake City's sole private country club and was founded in 1910 by Tacoma businessmen who brought their canoes to American Lake. *Courtesy of Sharon Montgomery.*

> *We take the Pacific Traction line in reaching our camp. The Northern Pacific has three stations on the lake. They are Country Club, American Lake and Murray, in the order in which they come when coming from Tacoma. Murray is located on Murray Creek and about one-fourth mile from the lake. Camp Stanley, the summer maneuvering grounds of 6,000 federal troops and militiamen is near Murray…*
>
> *The only park on the lake is called Traction Park and is owned by the Pacific Traction Company. It is a beautiful park, located just south of Lake City. The park forms a fitting terminal for their line. Boating, swimming, a merry-go-round, three shooting galleries and sports compose the list of amusements.*
>
> *The beaches of the lake are few…some agates may be found along the beach, but they are all very small.*
>
> *From our camp an excellent and unexcelled view of Mt. Tacoma may be had on any clear day. The view is quite different from that obtained from the city. The mountain looks larger, and each of the three peaks surrounding the summit is plainly visible.*
>
> *The mountain looks blue during the larger part of the day, changing to a beautiful pink toward evening, and to purple late in the evening, and finally to a dim gray at night.*

A 1909 *Tacoma Ledger* story reported that Howard Gregory, author of the Lakeside Country Club diary, saved ten-year-old Harley Garrison, who was bathing in the lake. His cries for help were heard by Gregory, who swam to the boy's assistance without stopping to remove his coat or shoes, reaching him just in time.

Gregory dismissed any praise, the article said, adding that he and his sister were both excellent swimmers.

Once a guest enters through the impressive black wrought-iron gate, a meandering path bordered by rhododendrons and evergreens winds across the property toward the shoreline, with walkways to each home and a path to the clubhouse at the edge of the lake. In the winter, during the holiday season, the lampposts are decorated with greenery and ribbons.

THE CITY THAT NEVER WAS

By Rod Cardwell

According to this 1961 *Tacoma News Tribune* article, Lake City never was a city; instead, in the early 1960s, it was relegated to suburb status. How did the city that seemed to have a glorious future ahead of it dwindle to a neighborhood, divided by the winding route of Veteran's Drive?

Awakened by crowbar, hammer and saw, the ghosts have come to play at the edge of American Lake.

Once the old building stood for the lifeblood of America: the two-room school, bell in the tower calling the boys and girls from their hide and seek, chalk dust stinging the nostrils as the hickory stick stung the stubborn and the lazy.

Once a great destiny was envisioned for Lake City where the tourists came by railroad and a 50-passenger steamer plied its wake. "The air has a delightful fragrance," the passengers boasted, "especially for sufferers of hay fever and rose fever, whose afflictions seem to vanish when on it."

The Tacoma and Lake City Railroad and Navigation Co. would run tracks all the way to the Columbia and into Oregon. Nothing was impossible. Lake City's future was unlimited.

The ghosts have been stirred by the dismantling of a wooden building on the grounds of Lake City Elementary School.

In the "Gay Nineties" the building probably was the community's first school. From old clippings and remembrances, history-minded residents have determined that the building was the center of learning as far back as 1894.

It probably was a school in 1891; the year formal education came to Lake City. Some residents are not sure but that the building had been used elsewhere and was moved to the community.

At any rate it was a part of the Lake City School District, officially established in 1892, and in operation until it was absorbed into the Clover Park School District in 1941. Mrs. Ivan (Sarah) Nelson of 8308 Steilacoom Ave. SW attended the school from 1907–1914, when it was abandoned.

She said the building was boarded up. She said the students were herded into a new building, described at the time as one of the finest school buildings on the west coast. It cost $13,000, a newspaper article about the dedication rites reported.

One night a year after it opened the new school was destroyed by fire. Back into brief use went the old school building. When another school was built, the old one was again closed, until 1930. That year the Lake City Community Club used publicly subscribed funds to build a structure a short distance and opened it as a community center.

Lake City residents voted there for Calvin Coolidge, John Cox, Al Smith, Herbert Hoover, FDR, Alf Landon, Wendell Wilkie. And it also was used as the home for WPA sewing classes, Townsend Club gatherings, a Sunday school and many other things.

It was the community club's meeting place for 38 years, and the members remodeled the interior. In 1958, a new clubhouse was built. The old building standing on the site was sold to the Lakewood Masonic Club. Now that organization has sold it to Charles L. Ashley. He is tearing it down for salvage. The Clover Park district has no use for the site.

Mrs. James (Rose) Parkinson of 8806 Newgrove Ave. SW was the community club's secretary (1957–58) and is an amateur historian. She would like to compile a history of the community and has tried to uncover specific details about the early days of the two-room school. She and Mrs. Nelson hope residents with more information will contact them.

Today Lake City is a generally quiet, beautiful neighborhood of the Lakes District. It is the gateway to the American Lake Veterans Administration Hospital, and during the warm season, this "city that never was" watches thousands pass through to the community park on the magnificent body of water.

In the '60s (the city) was in the news when national honors were heaped on Roy McKasson, a Lake City boy who went from Clover Park High to the University of Washington and fame as an All-American football player.

The ghosts aroused from the slumber of history by the razing of the old structure are of the golden days when the community had big dreams.

A 1956 article about the Lake District Improvement Council said that "it is believed that these successes [by the LDIC] inspired the Tenzler family to donate over a million dollars for the present Lakewood Library."

Lake City Community Church: It May Have Started with a Handkerchief and a Smile

Whatever the truth is to conflicting stories about how their grandparents met during their transatlantic voyage, there's no doubt that Joseph Holt and his wife, Mary, left their mark on the Lake City community.

View of Holt Chapel, Lake City. The chapel was built in 1923 by Joseph Holt and later incorporated into the current Lake City Community Church. *Author's collection.*

Holt's granddaughter Gloria Blair smiled as she recalled one account about lemons and oranges that had been passed down in her family.

That family legend says that when Mary spotted the seasick Joseph, she offered Joseph a concoction of lemons and oranges to settle his stomach.

According to Gloria's daughter Diane Kirby, though, the Holts did meet during their voyage to America: "Gramma was seasick and vomiting over the side. Grampa offered his hankie for her mouth. Then he said, 'Let me be your mirror and straighten your hat.' She thought that was romantic."

Although the Holts, their two daughters and one son settled on land at the west end of American Lake in 1908, after Tacoma businessmen decided to sell the property to the U.S. government to establish a military fort, they purchased other property in Lake City, where Mr. Holt built three houses. On property across Alameda Avenue, he donated three lots for the Holt Chapel, which eventually became the Lake City Community Church. Two more lots were donated through the Puget Sound Bank, and on this site the church complex now stands.

According to the Holts' records, "In January 1923 it's because of the love of the Lord Jesus Christ in Holt's heart for the souls of the boys and girls, and men and women in the area, that the Lake City Sunday School was organized."

Later that month, according to Diane Kirby, the Lend-a-Hand Society developed out of those Sunday school meetings, held in the home of Mrs. Phillip Gay. In July of that same year, ground was broken, and the excavation of the church basement was completed. The young congregation celebrated the Fourth of July by building the forms for the basement walls. An all-day picnic was held across the street from the church beneath the fir trees that still stand.

Mary Holt wrote:

> *In January 1927, the auditorium was dedicated. This was a memorable day in the hearts of many of us. For many years the work continued only as a Sunday school, with Christian Endeavor* [the youth program] *in the evenings, and the occasional speaker.*

In 1936, the first minister was hired. He earned twenty dollars per month. It was under his ministry that the need for a church organization was felt and that work began.

In 1945, under the ministry of Reverend Stan Johnson, the church was incorporated, and the name of "Lake City Church" was filed in Olympia. The constitution and articles of faith and covenant were adopted, and the church—to be known as a nondenominational church based solely on the teachings and doctrines of the New Testament—was formally established.

Four years later, a former navy barracks building was barged down the Puget Sound to Steilacoom from Bremerton and moved to the Lake City Church site, where it was used as a nursery and for Sunday school classes. A smaller building became the parsonage. A bus was purchased and a route established through Lakeview Village that transported an average of thirty-two riders to Lake City each Sunday. Two more buses were added, transporting an average of seventy-five riders to the church.

In 1955, the constitution was dated, and the church officially became the Lake City Community Church. As the congregation increased, it needed more room. Although Joseph had died of stomach cancer several years earlier, in 1954 Mary laid the cornerstone for the building. During a five- to six-year period, church members continued to work on the main sanctuary. Each Saturday during that time, the men worked while the women provided hot lunch. In 1957, the church was finally finished and dedicated.

In 1964, a group of boys playing with matches started a fire in the church, damaging the main sanctuary at a cost of $63,000. Fortunately, no one was hurt. During the next five months, church services were held at the Lake City Community Clubhouse. The following year, the restored sanctuary, along with a new educational wing, was dedicated.

A new foyer was added to the front of the sanctuary (along with a much-appreciated new ladies' restroom). The church celebrated its fiftieth anniversary in 1973, and in 2005, a gymnasium was added, providing a permanent home for the Bread of Life food bank, as well as plenty of room for a multitude of youth and adult activities.

As once was traditional in many areas around the country, the church and school continue to serve as focal points for the community through a variety of activities.

The church has met many challenges over the years, according to a 1957 *Suburban Times* article:

> *We must not judge a church by its building but by the fellowship, cooperation, devotion, love and search for the strength which has motivated this congregation and caused it to grow are wonderful forces for which our community may be thankful.*

Mr. Holt served as caretaker for the Lakeside Country Club.

The grave site of Mary and Joseph Holt, Old Settlers Cemetery. *Author's collection.*

The Holts are buried in an elevated plot in the Old Settler's Cemetery on Washington Boulevard, approximately a half mile from Lake City.

The Holts' side-by-side graves are topped with ornate marble tombstones: The engraved stones read, "Mary Anne Milne Marshall Ireland, born Dec. 31, 1881, died 1965" and "Joseph Holt, born Aug. 12, 1881, died 1945."

The Veterans' Affairs Hospital on American Lake

After the Civil War, many state veterans' homes were established. A new system of veterans' services were established when the United States entered World War I.

The establishment of the Veterans' Administration came in 1930, when Congress authorized the president to consolidate and coordinate government activities for war veterans.

Returning to the creation of the area now known as JBLM, the pre- election in Pierce County was set for January 6, 1917. After a successful election, the

American Lake site was purchased for a cantonment. Snow-clad Mount Rainier guarded its eastern horizon, and American Lake bounded it on the west.

A revocable license from the War Department, dated January 3, 1923, leased 377 acres of this land for the Veterans' Hospital on American Lake, which is said to have the most beautiful physical setting of all the Veterans' Administration hospitals. The remainder of the surrounding acreage includes wooded lands, approximately 91 acres in lawns, 25 acres in general farming, 5 acres in berries and approximately 60 acres for a nine-hole golf course. The soil is filled with rock fragments characteristic of glacial drift. The buildings, Spanish-American-type architecture, are nestled along a beautiful shoreline of 1.8 miles.

The description of the hospital's "most beautiful" setting echoes words written by Mary Bonney Shorey in the 1870s to describe the donation claim where her parents, Sherwood and Lydia Bonney, settled after coming to the area in the mid-1850s.

The history of the medical facility located in Lake City at the southern end of the road known as Veteran's Drive began in 1923, five years after the armistice was signed to end the Great War.

The facility was the ninety-fourth hospital to be built by the War Department for the provision of care for World War I veterans. The

Doctors' residences at American Lake Veterans' Affairs Hospital. *Author's collection.*

Hurley-Mason Company was awarded the contract for the construction of the facility. A site was chosen on the western shore of American Lake for construction of the hospital. Many of the stucco and terra-cotta buildings are listed on the National Register of Historic Places and are still enjoyed by patients and staff for their aesthetic beauty.

The medical center was dedicated in 1924 and chartered with a single mission: neuropsychiatric treatment. On March 15, 1924, the first fifty patients were transferred to the hospital from Western State Hospital at Fort Steilacoom.

Since 2003, the hospital has expanded its mission to treat traumatized veterans from recent wars in the Middle East. A nine-hole golf course, designed for patient rehabilitation, is just one of the latest additions to the site. A second course is scheduled to be added.

VA Hospital Property Landmarks

The solid-looking facility is approached by a meandering two-lane road that begins south of the hospital in Lake City, just off Gravelly Lake Drive. One side parallels the lake; the other parallels the golf course. The edge of Joint Base Lewis-McChord (originally Fort Lewis) seems to embrace the hospital's 377-acre site. A row of flagpoles lines the left side of the hospital's approach—fitting for a military medical treatment facility.

A pair of plain, wrought-iron lanterns sits atop opposite cobblestone columns that mark the entry to the Veterans' Hospital in Lake City. Occupational therapy patients early on in the hospital's existence crafted the lanterns, according to a history archived in Tacoma Public Library's Northwest Room. Numerous examples of items crafted by patients are encountered throughout the facility.

Over the years, the hospital has grown from its initial mission to that of a multicare facility. In the 1960s and '70s, ambulatory surgical services, a seventy-six-bed nursing home unit, blind rehabilitation services, a substance abuse treatment program and a sixty-bed homeless residence were added to the scope of care to veterans.

Additional special programs were added in the 1980s and '90s, such as vocational rehabilitation, a residential care program and a post-traumatic stress treatment program.

Building number 81 was renovated in 1998, with an addition that allowed for relocation and expansion of primary care and a women's health clinic.

Ongoing remodeling, upgrading and expansion of the facilities will occur while preserving the historic character of this campus.

In 2024, the hospital will mark its centennial.

Chapter 4

HAPPENINGS ON AND AROUND AMERICAN LAKE

American Lake's "ET" Visitor

According to a headline story in the July 17, 1928 edition of the *Tacoma Daily Ledger*, fragments of a meteor were found on the grounds of the Tacoma Country and Golf Course, questionable evidence that late on the previous evening, around midnight, a blazing ball of metal had been seen, streaking across the sky above American Lake.

The news article's sub-headline said that the metal was "conclusive proof of heavenly visitor's nearness to Tacoma shown by pieces picked up on the golf course."

And furthermore, a "City Commission figures the mass hit within 20 miles of the area."

Geology instructor F.A. McMillan, from the University of Puget Sound's (UPS) newly established department, examined the pieces found on the golf course and declared they were likely "pieces of sporadosiderite, or meteorite, consisting of metallic oxides."

An accompanying news story on the front page reported about a meteor seen streaking across the state before crashing near Aberdeen.

Supposedly, those fragments were stored at UPS, but recent efforts to track down the cache left behind by this mysterious meteor were unsuccessful. Indeed, current UPS geology professor Jeff Tepper said he'd never heard about the collection. So evidence of this strange celestial visitor remains a mystery to this day.

Jim Hammond and Dick White's Float Plane Base on American Lake

Of all the maritime traffic that plied American Lake, perhaps none is as unique as that of the floatplanes, or flying boats, that took off and landed on the lake during a fifty-year period beginning in the late 1940s and continuing until 1999. Although the formal seaplane rental business has been relocated to Commencement Bay—in response to alleged complaints by lake residents after Lakewood incorporated as a city in 1996, instituting a variety of regulations and codes—the seaplane base at Lake City Park was closed. According to the city's website, however, the lake may still be used as a seaplane landing site if/as needed. The city's parks and recreation department manager is designated as the official contact person should a seaplane wish to land there.

Jim Hammond and Dick White were the original owners of the American Lake Seaplane Base. According to an August 24, 1947 story in the *Tacoma Daily Ledger/News Tribune* written by reporter Howie Clifford:

> *One of the newest flying services in this area is the Lake Aero Service, Inc., operator of the American Lake Seaplane base. The organization was incorporated in January of this year, and a few weeks later purchased the property on the north shore of the lake. The site is on Veterans Drive next to the old Martin Boathouse (circa 1920s) and the tract includes 150 ft. of waterfront and goes back to the road, a distance of 500 ft.*
>
> *Operators of the corporation were Jim Hammond, president, and Dick White, Vice President and treasurer. Both operators were residents of the Lakes District and during the winter months were A&E instructors at the Clover Park Vocation School. Both men picked up their mechanic ratings while working for Pan American before the war, and Jim served as an aviation machinist's mate, first class, during the conflict.*
>
> *Dick also held an instructor's ticket in teaching air students in the tricks of the trade in the outfit's float-equipped Piper Cub. White also was a CAA maintenance instructor in the area, while Hammond has an application in at the present time for the same rating.*
>
> *Facilities at the base consisted of an office and ramp with a large concrete hangar under construction. Further facilities plans include another hangar, equipment, picnic and parking facilities on the higher ground and numerous other attractions for the entire family. Gas and oil are available as*

Aerial view of Lake City. *Tacoma Public Library.*

> *are limited repairs with the corporation operating a full time repair service at the Lakewood Airport, with LeRoy Johnson in charge.*
>
> *Transportation to town is to be had, and the lake is able to handle landings and take offs in any direction, there are no runway troubles. Altitude is approximately 250 ft.*

A scaled-down model of a De Havilland seaplane that "soars" over the tables in the cocktail lounge at Bur's Restaurant on Steilacoom Boulevard is a replica of the seaplane that the last, and now retired, American Lake/Lake City seaplane base operator Bob McMahon once flew. He often "parked" his full-sized floatplane on Lake Steilacoom, just at the edge of his lakefront home. Bob explained that the model was a promo for Canadian Mist. The model originally was hung in the Harvester Restaurant in Tacoma's Stadium District until McMahon convinced the owners it should be displayed in Lakewood.

Between 1982 and 1999, McMahon operated the Hammond-White business that began in 1947 on American Lake near the site of present-day American Lake Park.

McMahon's seaplane interest developed because, he said, "he liked to make model airplanes." One thing led to another, and the youth, who was a student in the Clover Park School District between 1945 and 1956, met instructor Dick White in the late '40s. McMahon wanted to fly.

From his paper route, delivering the *News Tribune* to subscribers around the Lake Steilacoom neighborhood, McMahon had saved enough to pay for about ten hours of flying instruction before he could be certified. Lessons cost eleven dollars per hour.

"That included gas and instruction," he added.

McMahon's Seaplane Base

An early 1990s *News Tribune* photo shows a young man, attired in a tuxedo, who arranged with McMahon to fly him and his prom date to a Tacoma waterfront restaurant. The story recapped the newsworthy event.

In the 1920s, the American Lake Park site served as the setting for an amusement park, hotel/dance hall and boat launch. For about twenty years, Mr. Martin operated a boat launch at the site.

Bob McMahon with his seaplane at American Lake. *Courtesy of Bob McMahon.*

The county bought old Martin's Resort from Oscar Zeigler in May 1955. In the 1900s, it had been a popular recreation setting.

Several of Lakewood's prominent citizens encouraged the Pierce County commissioners to acquire the property, with the understanding that money would be raised in Lakewood and the Lakes District to finance the development of a public park.

Rex Kelly became president of the Lake City Community Club and appointed Clary Holm as park chairman. In 1955, Holm became president of the club. He began spending money for a dredge to remove all the old pilings and other debris from the site. (There is no word of whether he ever found the champagne bottle that Allen C. Mason had reportedly tossed in the water about sixty years earlier.) Truckloads of sand, donated by the Holroyd Gravel Company, were brought to the beach. Old streetcar tracks were donated for use as a fence around the site. Holm and Art Carden built the dock and diving tower, and the Lake City Club bought two Olympic-type diving towers and picnic tables. Everyone was disappointed when the county took out the dock a couple years later. The park was in use during the summer of 1955.

Bob McMahon was the final owner of the seaplane site.

After Lakewood was incorporated in 1996, the city tried to break the twenty-year lease that McMahon had with the county. He says he spent about $10,000 fighting the city, which finally dropped the lawsuit. Three years later, however, McMahon retired.

Until 1999, though, he kept between fourteen and fifteen planes tied down at the site. He'd devised a hydraulic lift to move planes around on site and had covered hangars built for the planes, enabling the mechanics to work under cover during winter months. He had problems with vandalism to planes, and boaters using the boat launch site often drove into the water.

His business encompassed the state from the Columbia River to Canada. Bob offered sightseeing tours to guests from Japan, Germany and other foreign countries. One German passenger, enthused about taking flying lessons, went home disappointed after McMahon convinced him that there was really no place in Germany to land a seaplane. Usually, he flew his guests up the Washington coast to Canada. Often, he flew "bird surveys" for the Washington State Game Department.

After a fire broke out in the Oakbrook area, on the far west side of Steilacoom Boulevard, McMahon flew the fire chief over the area so he could "direct the firefighters on the ground." The men truly had a bird's-eye view of that operation, he said.

Eventually, the seaplane base was closed because of residents' complaints about noise from the planes. The site became American Lake Park and today includes a boat launch, shelter, picnic tables and a swimming area. It's almost opposite Harry Todd Park on the lake's east side.

THE BOAT SHOE AVIATOR

The following poem, by aviator Bob Hamilton, captures the romance of flying a seaplane, courtesy of Bob McMahon:

THE BOAT SHOE AVIATOR
by Bob Hamilton

Boat shoe aviators, if it were honestly shown
Have seen more wilderness than others have known

Be it flying boat or floatplane, most people agree
The seductive wilderness they are best able to see

For the seaplane is a magic carpet, we've been told,
To the supernatural land where it often gets cold

And where rock and blue-streaked glaciers abound
In the awesome sky-shredding mountains of the Sound

They say once you have flown to this land unnamed
You'll never ever again be quite the same

You won't give a damn, for pilots of a lower standing
Who fly planes capable of only one water landing

Other pilots may hangar-fly, talking of this & that
But you'll see pristine lakes and a rainbow fat

You may enjoy being with your wife & smile at her
But you'll hear the loon's call & the wind in the fir

For once you've been captivated by a sea-plane
You'll never again be quite the same.

In the June 10, 2013 edition of the *News Tribune*, it was announced that a new seaplane float "may enhance Tacoma's transportation identity." Reporter John Gillie wrote that "Tacoma last week joined a select group of cities with a special aviation asset adjacent to their downtown."

This new site is near the Foss Waterway. Greg Corrado, vice-president of the Washington Seaplane Pilots Association, said the association was developing procedures to minimize noise and to ensure that seaplanes would be considered good neighbors. Seaplane visits are likely to be intermittent, not like regular operations from such popular Northwest destinations as Victoria's Inner Harbor and Vancouver's Coal Harbor.

News from Tillicum

An assortment of news clippings, pasted in a pair of large brown scrapbooks, made up an informal history of Tillicum, assembled for the community's 2010 centennial celebration. A few highlights with references to Tillicum landmarks include the Lahoma Inn, where Mrs. Jessie West served her famous chicken dinners as early as 1917. Bill's Boathouse, the Bar-B-Q Inn and Bona's IGA were also mentioned.

According to a 1972 news article, at that time the community had a population of 1,400; by 2010, that figure had grown to 2,100. At one time in the 1980s, according to Jim Taylor, longtime resident (he was born in Tillicum in 1933), the population was 3,000, and residents petitioned the county to be incorporated. But former Pierce County executive Joe Stortini denied the request.

At that time, the community fire services were provided via the Lakes District Fire Department (forerunner of Lakewood's Fire Department), originally located on Gravelly Lake Drive, across from the high school.

In 1920, according to another news article, Mrs. Norman (Lucille) Harris's grandmother, Mrs. Jessie West, helped named Tillicum, a Chinook word for "friend." Mrs. Harris's great-aunt and grandmother both came to the area in 1885 and homesteaded on what became Camp Murray and, later, Fort Lewis. Jessie moved to Tillicum in 1910.

In her recollections, Mrs. Harris recalled Tillicum when it was a small community of residents who worked side-by-side. Regarding the beach, she remembered that the lake water "was much higher" at the time—about eight to ten feet higher. People came from all over to swim and sit on the beach.

LAKEHOMA INN—Chicken dinners were a specialty of Mrs. Jessie E. West who used to feed many people at her house, called Lakehoma Inn on Maple Street in Tillicum as early as 1917. Henderson's Store, about 150 feet away from the Inn was the village center of attraction.

A newspaper illustration, circa 1917, of the Lakehoma Inn, Tillicum, where Mrs. Jessie West served her famous chicken dinners. *Tacoma Public Library.*

"Marshmallow roasting was popular then, and people crowded the shorelines 'body to body' during the Word War I era," she said.

Mrs. Harris also recalled that some navy personnel trained at Camp Murray; they wore blue uniforms and white hats.

As a swimming area, the lake was popular but dangerous. As a young girl, she remembered watching divers retrieve drowned bodies, wrapping them in blankets and stacking the bodies on the porch of N.B. Henderson's store until they could be collected and taken away for burial. She recalled that she "couldn't stand to watch it." The death rate from drowning from 1915 to 1917—due in part to the "underwater currents"—was quite high, "but people kept on swimming." (Mr. Taylor, however, said that the lake is spring fed—there are no currents.)

Brown's Boathouse eventually was sold to Mr. Garrison, next to Don Gawley, then to Bill Merritt and ultimately to Glenn Anderson. In the '20s, the boathouse had a "chute to chute," where swimmers would enter the lake via a long slide toward Silcox Island. Today, the Andersons own property on Silcox Island.

Harry Bona's IGA grocery store was a popular gathering place in 1920. It was furnished with a pot-bellied stove and a cracker barrel, where customers would wait for the Tacoma trolley to arrive.

People traveled from as far away as forty miles to patronize Tait's Pavilion—the largest building in the area. Dances were held there on weekends. Patrons paid a nickel per dance; it's said that $100 was raised on a weekend. Until the pavilion burned down in the 1930s, it remained a popular dance site. The Tait family owned the pavilion and also owned

Churchill Enterprises. The Taits relocated to the Philippines, where they were taken prisoner during World War II.

From Calexico, Mexico, to the Canadian border, U.S. 99 was the West Coast's version of Route 66. Although not as widely celebrated as the famous cross-country "mother road" route to Los Angeles, nevertheless, Old 99 contains just as many interesting sights along its length.

After I-5 opened for business in the late '60s, Old 99 was demoted to what writer William Least Heat-Moon termed "blue highway" status (designated on maps by the color blue). Pieces of Old 99, however, still meander through its communities, such as Tillicum, Centralia and South Tacoma Way.

As the narrator in the Pixar movie *Cars* laments, "The road rose and fell with the land, all it did was save ten minutes of driving, changing people's driving habits to get some place 'faster'—they don't know what they're missing."

For non-highway travelers, the meandering road is still a preferred route for those living in communities bisected by the asphalt path, such as South Tacoma Way and Ponders.

Tillicum's community center at 15114 Grant Avenue was reputed to have had the best dance floor in the nation. The property was sold to Ken Rowe in 1970 and remodeled into a residence.

That popular dance hall was once transformed into a skating area by Adolph H. Reid, who donated his money to the youths of the village. Reid also sponsored many basketball teams and bought ham and pop for the teams.

Although Mr. Bona cleaned and maintained the area behind his store, that land was absorbed into what became known as Harry Todd Park—named for Mr. Todd, a Tacoma businessman who contributed three hundred feet of waterfront area, along with $100,000, to Tacoma's Metro Parks District.

Harry Todd Park, Tillicum. *Author's collection.*

The park was, to Mr. Taylor's knowledge, a swimming area for about forty years before it was renamed as Harry Todd Park. It was composed of Tillicum's swimming area and parkland donated by Mr. Bona. Mr. Todd paid for construction of the park pavilion. Jim Taylor recalled going to Bill's Boathouse to fish in the '40s.

The trolley stop was near Bona's (coming up from Highway 99). Bona gave parkland to Pierce County in the '60s, with the provision that it could not be sold or used for anything other than a park.

After Tillicum was designated as a City of Lakewood neighborhood, the park was transferred to the city's ownership. Today, it is the location for the Commencement Bay Rowing Club, as well as the University of Puget Sound (UPS) and Pacific Lutheran University (PLU) rowing clubs at the park's shell house. The shell house is where the clubs' racing shells are stored between races in vertical berths several levels high.

The present-day community center on Washington was constructed in 1984. It includes a small library, medical office and community meal site. Originally the community's library was located in Tillicum Elementary School. In 2012, the meal site collected thirteen thousand pounds of food donations. Mr. Taylor did some masonry work on Tillicum Elementary in 1952 and again in 1972.

In 1926, one of the most unusual sights was the floating pavilion that was moored near where Bill's Boathouse is today. The dock was roped to the land to prevent it from floating away.

Smith's Market, Tillicum. *Tacoma Public Library.*

With the 2014 baseball season officially underway, Tillicum sent its own newly organized team into the fray. The Tillicum team lineup included youngsters ranging in age from seven to eight, wearing bright orange T-shirts and ball caps to indicate they were members of the newest Little League team in Lakewood: the "Tillicum Crushers." Although their first game was rained out, it did not dampen the boys' enthusiasm.

Dave Anderson, president of the Tillicum Neighborhood Association, roused the community to support the effort, garnering financial support from community businesses to outfit the players, with assistance from Tillicum Elementary School.

American Lake Want Ad

A classified ad from a May 1911 edition of the *Tacoma Times* read:

> *American Lake*
>
> *Overlooking the water, a place where you can make yourself independent. This place is used for a hotel and restaurant. There is* [sic] *10 steady boarders now, the owner says she has had as many as 40 for dinner. To make this a moneymaker, you can run a grocery store in connection, as a store is badly needed. It is a large, seven-room house, beautifully located, with good size tract of land, fruit trees, flowers and shrubbery of all kinds, nice oaks and small firs surround the place. You can get this place for $1800. Will take part trade.*

Alice V. (Anderson) Nelson, formerly of Tillicum, provided this ad. During the 1990s, Nelson was editor/publisher of the *Tillicum Times*, a monthly publication for Tillicum residents.

A Few More Tillicum Tales

> *August 17, 1924: One of the largest picnics of the year, to be held at Garrisons, is the Pierce County Courthouse Picnic. A large program of both field and water sports, a tug-of-war, boat, canoe, swimming and foot racing, has been arranged. A special dance in Garrison Pavilion will also be held Saturday evening.*

A June 19, 1925 *Tacoma Daily Ledger* article reported:

> *Ray Tingrey, young welterweight, who is returning to the ring after a year lay-off, and Ray Small, light weight, will work out Sunday afternoon at Garrison's Place on American Lake Southside; other boxers will also give visitors to the park an idea of how fighters train for battle.*

In July 1956, the hydroplane *Miss Tacoma*, a Seafair Regatta hopeful, hit the water at American Lake but was quickly removed to dry land because of a leaky pit line.

Displacing U.S. 99 in the early 1960s with I-5 had an impact on residents of the Woodbrook and Tillicum areas. Once the railroad tracks had been removed, two brothers petitioned the county to rename the road Railroad Avenue. Now, Burlington Northern/Santa Fe Railroad wants to replace those tracks. The reason for using the name Union Avenue adjacent to Washington Avenue was to be consistent with Tacoma's Union Avenue.

Old Highway 99, Jim Taylor remembered, continued from Gravelly Lake Drive onto what is now the freeway and beneath the current underpass up to Thorne Lane. The small community is literally landlocked. Access to Tillicum is solely via the Thorne Lane or the JBLM exit from I-5. There is, however, emergency-only access through the country club property.

The Bar-B-Q Inn, Tillicum's most well-known restaurant in its day, was relocated across the road but remains closed.

Bar-B-Q Inn, Tillicum, circa 1931, along Old Highway 99, which was replaced with I-5 in 1964. *Tacoma Public Library.*

Tillicum Elementary School was built in the early 1940s. Before that school was built, students from the area attended a school known as American Lake South. Since it was built in 1943, Tillicum Elementary School has been a hub for the community it serves. Students, staff, families and community members continue to work in partnership to help students learn and be successful and for the community to thrive. Its current principal is Taj Jensen.

Dave Anderson, Tillicum resident and neighborhood association president and editor/publisher of the Tillicum/Woodbrook neighborhood newsletter, recently published an article memorializing Tillicum Elementary teacher Luella Johnson, who passed away on March 21, 2014. In his tribute to Mrs. Johnson, David Anderson wrote, "Truly, everything I needed to know, I learned in her Kindergarten." David explained how he and Mrs. Johnson shared the same birthday—decades apart, of course.

He concluded by asking:

> *Is not the greatest object of education to inspire the student by way of the passionate teacher's opening of the window to the world and, in that glimpse of possibilities, help them see what they could be; that their momentary unintelligible scribbles will one day have great significance and that the journey of discovery begins now?*

One of the biggest events at the south end of American Lake South, according to an article in the *Lakewood Log* of 1937, was the annual picnic for the regional division of Puget Sound Power and Light Company. The yearly gathering was held at the twenty-acre site adjacent to Camp Murray for Puget Sound Power and Light employees from Kent to Kelso. Activities included lectures, sports and field games.

In 1996, it was converted to a fifty-six-home retirement community named Eagle Point.

Ken Hill, the caretaker, had managed the site for fourteen years. He recalled the camping days when his family came there to fish, swim, boat, sunbathe and toast marshmallows over the campfire. After the property was sold, he and his wife "moved on."

Camp Murray was named for the Murray family, who had homesteaded on the land prior to World War I. Today, it is the site of the Washington National Guard headquarters.

Shades of James Bond

Tillicum's centennial scrapbook included a photo of a 1962 amphi-car with a top speed of seven miles per hour. Built in Germany and featured in an early Bond film, it was the only amphibious car to be mass produced—3,878 were built. Taylor says there are now three amphi-cars used by Silcox Island residents.

Mr. Taylor's parents came to the area from Pennsylvania and Missouri. His father began a construction company. Jim took over its operation in 1971. His son owned it until 2008, when recession impacted the business and it closed.

Taylor attended Clover Park High School (he's one of the Ancient Warriors) and recalls working on building many places around the area, such as at Lakewold Gardens, Tacoma's County/City building, brickwork on the old Puget Sound Hospital, several schools (including Tillicum Elementary) and the Tacoma Greyhound station on Pacific Avenue.

THE DEVELOPMENT OF CAMP LEWIS

Tacoma historian Murray Morgan wrote in his book *Puget's Sound* that Tacoma's mayor, Angelo Fawcett (whose political career was erratic), "achieved his greatest triumph during his third term through the creation of Camp Lewis."

According to Morgan's account, in September 1916, Steve Appleby, a cashier at the National Bank of Tacoma (Thorne's bank), attended an encampment of the National Businessmen's Preparation League at American Lake. From the military grapevine, he picked up the rumor that the War Department had sent Captain Richard Park to Seattle to study sites in the

Pacific Northwest for an army encampment but that nothing near Tacoma was under consideration. "No banker could fail to see the injustice of that oversight," he said. He alerted his peers, who descended on Captain Park in sufficient strength, "pressuring" him to tour the area around American Lake. Morgan reports:

> *He was as impressed as Dr. Tolmie and Lieutenant Wilkes had been. General J.F. Bell, commanding general of the Western Department came up from San Francisco. He found the land good but expensive. Bell, without making any commitment, let it be known that if they could acquire say, 30,000 acres, they might establish a post. The promise to use local materials for its construction sweetened the deal. When the Army found that Tacoma-Pierce was eager for the deal, they raised the offer to 110,000 acres; but eventually settled for 70,000 acres.*
>
> *In December 1916, Fawcett proclaimed Tacoma's need for the military presence. He sponsored a drive among local businessmen to raise funds to pass a bond issue under which the Pierce County citizens would pledge $2 million to the federal government—ironically, it was land that the federal government had given to the state to give out to private citizens.*

Before the vote could be taken, however, America declared war, and the U.S. government took the land and began construction of Camp Lewis, later Fort Lewis. Captain David Stone, quartermaster, was responsible for the fort's construction. Using local lumber, it's said that it was the only military camp ever to be built in such a short time.

In October 2014, Historical Societies from Tacoma and Lakewood plan to partner in the annual Destiny Dinner that will be held on American Lake at JBLM's event center (originally the NCO Club). The occasion? To commemorate the centennial of World War I and Tacoma's role in that fort.

Camp Lewis was created in 1917 after the United States entered World War I. Quartermaster captain David Stone was the driving force behind construction of the camp. The camp was constructed quickly and was the least expensive army camp built during the war. *Library of Congress.*

BILL'S BOATHOUSE AT TILLICUM

A news article in the June 15, 1924 edition of the *Tacoma Sunday Ledger* featured a photo of Garrison's Boat House, announcing it had modern equipment. Adjacent to the boathouse was a long ramp/slide down which adventurous swimmers could "chute" into the lake—i.e., a long water slide, forerunner of contemporary water park chutes and tunnels. The caption announced that Garrison's had the finest equipment "as regards canoes and rowboats to be found anywhere on the Pacific Coast." The photo illustrates

> *some idea what to expect when a canoe is ordered and so no privately owned boat could be more beautiful or serviceable.*
>
> *Mr. Garrison now has about the only ground available for the use of the public to be found on American Lake where picnics can be held and where the*

Washington's Playground

Lake Resort Has Model Equipment

A *Tacoma Sunday Daily Ledger* article about Garrison's Boat House in Tillicum (forerunner of Bill's Boathouse). *Tacoma Public Library.*

> *facilities for enjoying oneself are so complete. A road is being developed along the waterfront and a grandstand is under construction from which the public may view in coming weeks the several swimming meets which will be held there this summer. The many improvements which Mr. Garrison has in mind, when completed, will make this spot the most modern playground in the Northwest.*

According to a recollection from the Silcox Island centennial book, in 1932 or 1933, a float and diving tower were moved from the old Garrison's Swimming Resort west three hundred feet by Don Gawley, who built a new boathouse.

Prior to the '30s, a man named Mr. Brown had operated the original boathouse, which has since evolved into the current business. When a big windstorm blew up in 1934, the fishermen weren't able to get off the lake in time to miss the huge waves that made their boats disappear from the sight of those watching from on shore. The downed trees damaged many of the cars in the parking lot.

In the '40s, Garrison built a large float so it could be used for dances, special events such as the Fourth of July and other affairs. The next owner was Don Gawley, who sold the boathouse to the Merritt-Thomas Corp in 1945, and it became known as "Bill's Boathouse," according to Dave Fogg.

Bill Merritt operated it until 1971, when it was sold to Glenn and Genevieve Anderson. Glenn was well known for restoring classic old boats, motors and cars.

Historic sign to Bill's Boathouse, Tillicum. *Author's collection.*

Carved statue of "Bill," Tillicum. *Author's collection.*

Anderson's son David also is involved with the restorations. David became boathouse operator after his parents passed away, and he is active in community politics—including publishing a regular community newsletter.

At the September 12, 2013 meeting of Lakewood United, David said that his father had long wanted to purchase a boathouse. So he did. Dave and his brother regularly helped with chores—cleaning boats, selling merchandise, etc.

One anecdote he shared was about the time his father and his assistant cleaned out the septic tank. It happened that the pipe was seriously plugged. Both Glenn and his assistant finally broke loose the stuck pipe, but afterward both men dove into the lake to remove the gunk!

Glenn arranged with the state to provide and keep the lake stocked with rainbow trout. There's a feeding pen on the site. Dave told about a rainbow that had survived over the winter in less than a foot of water. The hibernating rainbow was released into the lake.

Bill's boathouse hosts its own opening day of fishing every year.

David said that his dad always found a use for anything. For example, Glenn collected cast-off wood scraps, glued them together and created "paddles" that currently are on display around the Northwest at all Ram Restaurants. He also provided the paddle part for oars for the University of Oregon's crew teams.

David helped his father restore many boats. After Lakewood became a city in 1996, it wrangled with other jurisdictions in its efforts to make area businesses comply with its various codes, including signs.

One of these "battles" over signage had an impact on Bill's Boathouse, with the result that in 1999, a large, carved wooden figure, representing the mythical "Bill," was anonymously presented to Glenn. The yellow-coated bewhiskered figure has stood at the end of the property ever since, adjacent to an older sign encouraging folks to take their kids fishing. The Andersons have no idea who provided or created the statue of "Bill"—it's a replica of Glenn—but it has become a local landmark.

The boathouse consists of storage for rowboats, as well as an assortment of restored classic boats, and is adjacent to the staging area for Silcox Island residents' cars and boats.

A larger boathouse at Harry Todd Park shelters the racing shells for the University of Puget Sound, Pacific Lutheran University and the Commencement Bay Rowing Club. The lake's waters, considered to be some of the finest rowing waters in the country, are the setting for the annual PLU/UPS Meyer-Lamberth Cup races. In 2013, the schools hosted the fiftieth anniversary of that race.

Chapter 5

THE SHELL GAME

Rowing on American Lake

Ever since the first canoes traveled American Lake's length, hundreds of years before the British arrived, countless fishing boats, Ski-Doos and seaplanes have plied the lake's waters. Beginning in 1964, the lake became the setting for a collegiate competition. The regatta between the two local private colleges is the oldest annual dual regatta on the West Coast of the United States.

On April 13, 2013, four sleek racing hulls, powered by athletic young rowers from Pacific Lutheran University and the University of Puget Sound, flew over the waters from the Lake's North End to Harry Todd Park as these two local universities met to determine the latest winner of a fifty-year-old tradition known as the Meyer-Lamberth Cup. Early on that blustery, soggy April morning, rowers and fans arrived at Harry Todd Park on Tillicum's west side and staked out their spot to watch the fiftieth annual "rowing" of the Meyer-Lamberth Cup. Dozens of vehicles filled the park's lot, with auto overflow lining the road outside the park.

Cheers and chants ("UPS! UPS!" "Go Lutes!") rippled across the water from spectators standing on the park's hillside, including a tall logger mascot, accompanying the rowers in their gray-and-crimson or black-and-gold uniforms as they hoisted their shells and marched their crafts to the dock.

In unison, the rowers stepped from the dock into position and maneuvered their vessels into the middle of the lake before rowing to the north end for the race's start. Although the first rowers were out of sight around the corner of

American Lake Boathouse, at Harry Todd Park, serves the University of Puget Sound, Pacific Lutheran University and Commencement Bay Rowing Club. *Author's collection.*

the lake for the first portion of the two-thousand-meter event, once the first shell rounded the corner, spectators began cheering. The UPS fans' cheers grew even louder when UPS's boat crossed the finish line first.

Once all six races were completed, winners gathered at the boathouse to accept their trophies: cups for the Meyer and Lamberth races, as well as the Little Lamberth and Mini-Meyer. Trophies also were awarded for the Neil's Cup and Johnson's Cup.

During the race's half century of competition, the record up to 2013 was: PLU, 29; UPS, 21 (with UPS winning twelve of the last twelve regattas, including the 2013 event).

The *Husky Clipper* on American Lake

The "rest of the regatta story" was found on Wikipedia. According to a Wikipedia entry, PLU's crew received national notoriety in 1967, when the University of Washington requested that PLU return its old shell the *Husky Clipper*. That was the famous shell that the Huskies had used to win at the 1936 Olympics in Berlin. (The *Clipper* is featured in the 2013 book *The Boys in the Boat* by Daniel James Brown.)

In exchange, UW arranged for the Green Lake Crew to donate a shell, the *Loyal Shoudy*, to the PLU team. Faced with no means of transporting the *Shoudy* from north Seattle to PLU's home course in Parkland, team commodore and captain Jim Ojala devised a plan for the team to transport the shell from Lake Union through the Ballard Locks and down Puget Sound to the Tacoma Narrows.

After several months of endurance training, contacting the navy and U.S. Coast Guard and obtaining a parade permit to walk the shell through North Seattle from Green Lake to Lake Union, the ten team members prepared to embark on their journey. The stunt resulted in the team's receiving coverage of the event from the *Seattle Post-Intelligencer* newspaper, as well as national rowing magazine *Rowing News*.

The *Shoudy* was named for Dr. Loyal Shoudy, a fanatically loyal UW alumnus who established the tradition of the Shoudy Banquet. When the team won a regatta, Shoudy took the rowers to New York and treated them to a show and a gala dinner. Each boy found a ten-dollar bill at his plate, along with a purple tie. Shoudy continued the end-of-year tradition for decades.

The *Shoudy* saw action on American Lake for several seasons, according to former PLU rowing coach Dave Peterson. In 1970, the shell was sold to Washington State University for its growing crew program. Sadly, the *Shoudy* was wrecked on the rocks in the Snake River near Pullman. All that was saved was the hull, which was mounted and hung on a wall in the school's boathouse.

A footnote about racing shells in the Lakewood area: brothers Dave and Jeff Iverson now lead the Ram International operation. When Jeff Iverson (Jeff and Dave's father) was planning the Ruston Way restaurant (the first one in Lakewood opened in 1971), UPS contacted him and asked whether he wanted to purchase its wooden shell since it was switching over from wood to carbon fiber. The Ram took UPS up on the opportunity. Since that time, the Ram has hung the wooden shells in its restaurants as far away as Chicago.

"We always hang local high school banners from the oars," said Jeff Iverson.

Gallopin' with Gertie

Folks who drive to Tillicum—an I-5 off-road community formally established around 1910—do a "double-take when they spot the sign that advertises "Gallopin' Gertie's"

Is there possibly some connection with the infamous Tacoma Narrows Bridge that acquired that nickname in the 1940s, when high winds rushing

Antique cash register at Gallopin' Gertie's, Tillicum. *Author's collection.*

through the narrows caused the bridge to twist and turn and finally buckle and fall in the Sound?

Not so, according to Susan Rothwell, daughter of the famous Gertie Rice. Susan says that the restaurant all started in 1952, when Gertie took her son, David, for a haircut in Tillicum. Dissatisfied with the regular barber's technique, Gertie went to another shop instead and, in the process of searching for a barber, learned that the space next to the barber's shop was for rent.

Gertie thought it might make a nice variety store location, but the barber told her no; it was equipped to be used as a restaurant. Gertie decided that the price was right: forty-five dollars a month. Although Gertie had always worked in an office, she accepted the offer and opened Gertie's Grill—a one-woman hamburger joint. The business opened a few days before the Fourth of July. On the holiday, it was swamped with GIs. Gertie recruited her husband and children to help, and Gertie's Grill was off and running. Six years later, she bought a downtown Tillicum site—a former horse pasture—and opened her second location on March 17, 1958. Despite organized opposition from the community, she secured a Class H liquor license, expanded again in 1970 and converted a tenant's beauty parlor into a cocktail lounge.

The name, "Gallopin' Gertie's," had nothing to do with the notorious Tacoma Narrows Bridge that twisted apart in 1940. Instead, it honors Gertie's favorite pastime: betting on the nags that raced at Longacres. Gertie retired in 1978 (after twenty-six years in the business) and took up horse racing as her hobby.

Today, Susan and her sidekick, Rod, operate the renowned eatery. Step inside and take a look around: racing décor everywhere—from race-themed menu items to pony photos and from racetrack scoreboards to trophies. It's a popular, colorful '50s-style spot with a friendly atmosphere. Gertie's is a "home away from home" for the troops. Since the '60s, the troops have had a special place in their hearts for Gertie's.

As Susan says in her monthly newsletters—be sure to pick up a copy when you're there for lunch—"From Baghdad to Fort Lewis, you haven't been anywhere if you haven't been to Gertie's."

Susan became addicted to horses when she was ten. Even though she was supposed to be twelve before she was allowed to go to the track, Gertie fibbed about her age. She quickly became knowledgeable about the operation and some of the long-gone horses such as Cold Steel, whose trainer, Don Munger, now eighty, is still training horses in 2014.

Susan says she had her first riding lesson at Woodbrook. She fell off, got back on and later learned she'd cracked a rib.

Gertie, in partnership with Wayne Hill, owned a few racehorses. When people commented how much Gertie loved horses, Susan clarified, explaining that what Gertie "really liked was gambling. The horses were a way to do it."

Susan has since become a racehorse owner. "I have a lot of fun with the horses and designing our menu around them," she says. One day, she hopes to have a photo of her own horse in the Winner's Circle.

"I believe you should always, always 'run for the roses,'" she adds

Her newsletter, *Gallopin' with Gertie*, is a much looked forward to publication. Her observations and commentary about the community are on par with Neighborhood Association/Bill's Boathouse owner David Anderson's "no punches pulled" online paper, the *Tillicum/Woodbrook Neighborhood News.*

Off to the Races with Gertie

Susan Rothwell, owner of Tillicum's famous Gallopin' Gertie's Restaurant, kitty-corner from Camp Murray, publishes a newsletter each month for her customers. Following are excerpts from the April 2013 edition, No. 157.

According to *Gallopin' with Gertie*, Tillicum's 103-year-old history includes the following observation (advisory: this piece of local history may be a bit exaggerated since it was in her April Fools' edition):

Gallopin' Gertie's race hat restaurant sign, Tillicum. *Author's collection.*

> *The News that Amtrak is going full-speed ahead through Tillicum sent our historian digging to see how other trains fared in Tillicum history. Apparently not as well as they should have.*
>
> *According to early records, James Hill (aka The Empire Builder) was the last and greatest American Railroad leader who attempted to run a line around American Lake. In 1893, with circus-like fanfare, Tillicum welcomed Great Northern Railroad with open arms. Mr. Hill promised that no harm would come to Tillicum residents and indeed, the railroad would transform Tillicum into a vibrant productive region.*

An illustration showing a train wreck accompanied the article.

> *Despite flashing gates and blaring horns, trains collided. It was a giant mess. But, Mr. Hill was right about one thing: it did bring economic stability to Tillicum. Residents spent the next two years clearing the mess up, thus providing jobs for all 165 surviving residents.*

Tillicum today continues to wrangle with the railroad tracks that encroach on its business district, and ultimately the current freight-train-only service will be expanded to transport Amtrak passengers.

One Room and a Path: A Tillicum Woman's Recollections of Life on the Homefront During World War II

Have you ever served your family a "can can" dinner? (Hint: It's definitely not some gourmet French concoction.)

"Can can" dinners were a staple meal item during World War II, and one Tillicum resident, Virginia Maas, who often served meals created from some strange ingredients, included that recollection in her novel, *One Room and a Path*.

Blackouts, rationing and even culinary challenges were familiar to many who lived through that period when millions of Americans tightened their belts to help win the war.

Maas's patriotic contributions included taking a chance on starting a rental business. She wove those events into a novel that presents a glimpse into this bittersweet period about small-town "life on the homefront."

Jim Taylor with Virginia Maas celebrating her 100th birthday, 2013. *Courtesy of Erin Klas.*

Growing up at American Lake South, before I-5 was built, Virginia and John Maas married shortly after the war started and then bought a house and land not far from Camp Murray. The property also included several small wooden sheds.

The Tillicum homesite has been "home" for seventy years, Maas says, and this centenarian writer vowed that she will "never move."

"I'm going out feet first," she laughs.

Because many incoming GIs and their wives were desperate for accommodations in the '40s, the Maas family unexpectedly found themselves becoming landlords. Besides collecting rents, Maas also collected material for her someday-in-the-future novel.

Drawing on firsthand experience, Maas told the story through a series of flashbacks, beginning when her story's heroine, Maudie Cameron, learned that her husband, Charlie, had been injured at Fort Lewis. The flashback account began with the day she and Charlie launched their new rental enterprise.

Their first tenants were a young couple from Michigan who begged to rent the small backyard shed. Maudie, a novice in the business, reluctantly agreed. No sooner had the Michigan couple settled in than her second tenants, two men with jobs at the Tacoma Shipyard, asked to rent the other outbuilding. They'd been sleeping in their car, they told her. Finally, a persistent Fort Lewis housing representative reminded the Camerons about their "patriotic" duty, and they hesitantly leased their daylight basement to another desperate couple.

Over the months that followed, they experienced the peaks and valleys of their new enterprise, quickly learning that there was little to be done to evict unsatisfactory tenants who wouldn't pay on time and who trashed their quarters.

This reluctant landlady, though, dealt with situations from scorched curtains and gaudily repainted quarters to tenants who sneaked baths in her basement laundry tubs.

The story was balanced with glimpses of nature, too, such as the view from Maudie's kitchen window of dew-filled, lacy spiderwebs draping the branches of nearby firs.

The chapters are sprinkled with wry observations about the mandate to use ration stamps wisely and limit gasoline usage and the challenge of "making do" with limited ingredients for yet another "can" supper.

One memorable "can can" meal included the contents from a trio of unlabeled cans (a bargain at "ten cents each," she explained) of garbanzo beans, green beans and sauerkraut…and lots of bread. That "disastrous" dinner was saved by a quick trip down U.S. 99 to her parents' home to share their meatloaf and mashed potato dinner.

To fill her time while Charlie works at the PX, Maudie volunteered at Tacoma's USO Hall and shopped at Commerce Street's secondhand shops. She made time to shingle a neighbor's leaky roof and repair a leaky faucet. She also siphoned gas and changed a flat tire.

The discovery of an old letter stuffed inside the lining of a loveseat they were reupholstering sparked Maudie's doubt about her parentage.

"Am I a bastard?" she anxiously asked her mother. Check out the book to learn the answer. The audiobook of eight CDs is available from Pierce County Library.

Most memorable is Maudie's reaction after learning about her husband's heroic action, throwing himself on a frightened young soldier who was bent on destruction. The young GI, terrified about going overseas, decided to kill himself and his comrades rather than face certain death at the hands of the enemy.

Charlie acted as soon as the soldier pulled the grenade pin and ended up in Madigan's ICU. Fortunately, his brave act was not fatal.

Mrs. Maas, a freelance writer, not only wrote about her Tillicum homefront experiences, but she also authored numerous travel and feature articles for magazines and newspapers, including the *Tribune*. Because her name was

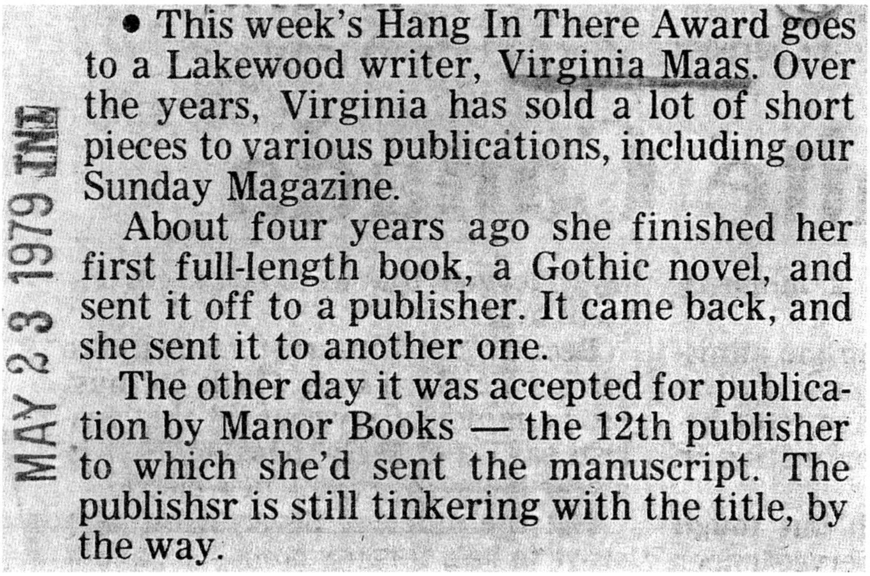

MAY 23 1979 TNT

• This week's Hang In There Award goes to a Lakewood writer, Virginia Maas. Over the years, Virginia has sold a lot of short pieces to various publications, including our Sunday Magazine.

About four years ago she finished her first full-length book, a Gothic novel, and sent it off to a publisher. It came back, and she sent it to another one.

The other day it was accepted for publication by Manor Books — the 12th publisher to which she'd sent the manuscript. The publishsr is still tinkering with the title, by the way.

An article about Virginia Maas, Tillicum author. *Tacoma Public Library.*

always included in the byline, her editor suggested she use a pseudonym for some of her stories.

The number of rejections she received for her novels, she laughs, would "paper a room."

At one time, she managed fifteen rental units; today, she manages five.

During the early days—the mid-1920s—of living in the American Lake community, Maas adds, "Tillicum was a small, homey town. Residents didn't lock their doors, and most of the men worked at the DuPont [explosives] plant."

Virginia still lives at her Tillicum home near Camp Murray. She recalled growing up on her parents' farm at nearby Woodbrook until she married her neighbor, John Maas, whose parents owned the adjacent farm. Later, the Maases owned a business in Ponders before moving to Tillicum.

The Return of *El Primero*

Castle owner Chester Thorne was interested in waterway development. He served as chairman of the Commercial Waterway District and was a member of the Union, University and Commercial Clubs, as well as the

Tacoma Country and Golf Club (golfing was his chief diversion). Thorne was a Republican, and Theodore Roosevelt and William H. Taft were both among guests entertained at his American Lake home.

Although he owned *El Primero*—he used it as a secure location for high-level national meetings, perhaps in the yacht's dining room or on the vessel's fantail—he was not a yachtsman. He is said to have enjoyed watching boats on American Lake. The yacht never did sail there.

He briefly was owner of the 1893 steam yacht *El Primero*, built in San Francisco for $250,000. Thorne is said alternatively to have lost the vessel in a poker game with *Tacoma Daily Ledger* publisher S.A. "Sam" Perkins and also to have been part owner in the vessel. *El Primero* became infamous in Tacoma maritime history, according to Tacoma historian Michael Sullivan. Perkins was said to have hosted many drinking parties aboard the 135-foot yacht (he was one-time commodore of the Tacoma Yacht Club). During World War II, the vessel was commissioned as a navy patrol boat. After the war, the yacht was used as a tour boat.

In late 2013, the still-impressive yacht briefly was moored at the Thea Foss Maritime Seaport Museum. "Chester Thorne" and "President W.H. Taft," portrayed by reenactors, were among the visitors that summer.

Chester Thorne purchased *El Primero* in 1906; it never sailed on American Lake, where he built his famous mansion. The 130-foot steam yacht was built in 1893 in San Francisco for $250,000. *Courtesy of Steve Wolff.*

Summer Fest Sponsors Hydroplane Races on American Lake

Between the late 1940s and the late 1960s, service clubs in the Lakes District hosted the annual Lakes Summer Fest. The event, held during the Fourth of July, included a parade with a decorated float featuring the current year's queen and princesses, an art exhibit, a barbecue picnic and boat races on American Lake. Jeanette Hurlow, the queen mother for 1969's events, shared details from her scrapbook of that year's event, including selection of the candidates and their outfits. Although most of the activities were held in Lakewood, the water events took place on American Lake. The event is known today as Summer Fest and usually takes place over a mid-July weekend at Fort Steilacoom Park.

Fishing with America's Warriors

At three thirty on the morning of July 13, 2013, John O'Reilly, Steilacoom's popular TopSide B&G owner, was in the bistro's kitchen whipping up pancake batter to feed a crowd of bass fishermen scheduled to show up at Russell Landing on JBLM later that morning for the Evergreen Bass Club's fifth annual outing, known as Fishing with America's Warriors.

It was definitely a glorious day for fishing!

O'Reilly's involvement came about because his business is conveniently located on the top floor of the Port Steilacoom Building, three floors higher than the Edward Jones office, where Al Lewis, the Bass Club's event coordinator, has his headquarters.

About three weeks earlier, as so often happens in this premier waterfront community when folks gather to chat, one thing led to another. The next thing John knew, he had volunteered to provide food for the Saturday outing. He is scheduled to reprise that role in 2014—and it's on its way to becoming another "Steilacoom tradition."

After making several phone calls, John lined up his food suppliers. Al recruited fellow Steilacoom Kiwanians, including John Inselman, Bob Mize, Harley Moberg, Ron and Jan Lucas, Doug Wing, George Phillips and more, to provide "people power," and the weekend fishing tourney was soon underway.

Hungry fishermen that morning chowed down on stacks of pancakes, sausages, coffee, cheese danishes and other tasty delights. Besides making

This rainbow trout is one of several species found in American Lake. Although the State of Washington periodically stocks the lake, Bill's Boathouse assists by nurturing some six thousand plus rainbows each year. The lake also contains yellow perch, large and small mouth bass and Kokanee trout. *United States Fish and Wildlife Service.*

the pancake batter, O'Reilly also whipped up some delicious root beer floats later on.

From 7:30 a.m. until noon, between twenty-nine and thirty warriors (representing all the services) and their families fished the length and breadth of American Lake—casting and catching trout, bass and more.

According to O'Reilly, the largest fish caught that day was a bass that weighed four and a half pounds—a weight that would surely make one longtime lake fisherman, Louis Raphael, really envious.

Everyone that day went home with something extra, such as an eastern Washington pheasant hunting trip, a spa massage and, last but not least, Jim Earl's famous fisherman's survival kit.

"Everyone wants to win that prize, so this year, we held it until last," Lewis explained.

Earl, a three-time Vietnam veteran, creates a new kit every year. It's a complete outdoorsman's survival outfit that includes a knife, rod and reel combo, tackle box, sleeping bag and survival kit.

There also were commemorative T-shirts, designed by Charles Davis of BluRoom Advertising. Larry Olson, of Rainier Apparel, had the shirts made up "at little or no cost to the bass club," Lewis said. A big "thanks" also went to Ed Sakai, who captured the action on film.

"This event was created five years ago," Lewis added, promising that "it will continue for one purpose and one purpose only. It's a short half day of fishing on the water, sponsored by the Evergreen Bass Club; just a short day for these brave young men and women who continue to serve everyday to keep our great country free."

Breakfast with the Ancient Warriors

The Ancient Warriors are a proud, supportive bunch of area residents with ties to Clover Park High School. According to a flyer provided at a breakfast gathering at Carr's Restaurant in Lakewood:

> *Anyone who attended or taught at Clover Park High School more than 50 years ago is ancient enough to be a member of the organization, and shall receive all of the following rights and privileges:*
>
> *Buy his/her own breakfast (fairly reasonable); Arrive at breakfast (if at all) as early or as late as he/she cares to without consequences on the dates noted below (Ancient Warriors meet around 8:30 a.m. every other Tuesday), and finally, refer to (or not) the words "Ancient Warrior" in his/her obituary.*

Ancient Warriors "founder" Jack Avril, CPHS '50 (John Fitzpatrick and Bob Brewer are also founders), says it "is a no-frills organization with no membership cards, or dues, no attendance records or secret handshake." Warrior "business" focuses on reminiscing about the good old days. The guys and gals have a good time, swapping "war stories" from their school and post-school days when they huddle in Carr's banquet room.

The Warriors began meeting around 1999, Avril said. The group is composed of CPHS classmates who graduated between 1947 and 1950. Many of them, such as Jim Taylor, Marvin Campeau, Parley Applegate, Alice Peeples and Harold Feaster, live in the Lakewood area; others are from farther away.

Almost two dozen of these ancients—at least a couple of them wearing green and white Warrior T-shirts—met on October 23 to talk about, among other things, the upcoming pigskin match between CPHS Warriors and SHS Sentinels, set for 7:00 p.m. on October 26 at Harry Lang Stadium.

Not surprisingly, several of these Ancient Warriors are former players—a lot of them in their late seventies or early eighties—and, as might be expected, a good bit of the conversation revolved around their days on the field.

"Remember the time you fell face down in the mud?" asked one former teammate.

"That's because my knee locked up!" the other replied. About ten years ago, he "finally" got around to having knee surgery.

These Warriors "support the school," said Don Ellingson, class of 1950 and the Warriors' "boss." They do so "by attending the games, [and] voting for the levies," and many planned to be at the game Friday night. Although there was no formal count of how many would show up at Harry Lang Stadium—Lang was a former CPHS coach, Ellingson added—"they're enthusiastic about the idea."

If it rains, the Warriors likely will remain in the stands instead of going onto the field.

After all, it's their presence that matters.

That evening, though, it rained, and Steilacoom won the game.

American Lake Post Offices

The earliest documented mail service in the lower Puget Sound region began in 1851. Mr. John Chapman served as mail carrier from Olympia while it was still part of Lewis County, Oregon Territory. He made one round trip per week, a total distance of twenty-eight miles one way. His compensation was not to exceed $2.70 per week.

Lake City Post Office was first established on August 18, 1890. It was discontinued on September 7, 1898, and moved to Lakeview.

Tillicum Post Office, established on March 12, 1908, was renamed "American Lake" on June 28, 1917.

"Old American Lake" at Lake City was reestablished on March 12, 1908, and then renamed "American Lake" on June 28, 1917.

The post office was located in a general merchandise store until it was moved directly across the street to Tillicum. It was discontinued in July 28, 1957, and moved to Tacoma. Early mail service to Tillicum was by a star route to Fort Lewis, Graham, Kapowsin, Electron and Ohop, but the last service was by star route Tacoma to Steilacoom.

The later American Lake post office was located in the Veterans' Hospital, and to differentiate between the two operations, the designation "old" was used.

In 2013, mail for Lake City and Tillicum was being distributed from the Lakewood post office, with the area's major distribution sorted at the Tacoma Plant on Pine Street.

Chapter 6

UNINCORPORATED PIERCE COUNTY

Separate Communities Become Lakewood Neighborhoods in 1996

EXCERPTS FROM THE *LAKEWOOD LOG*

After Lakewood newspaper publisher Charlie Mann launched his community newspaper in 1937, his weekly publication recruited residents for area communities such as Lakeview, Custer, Tillicum (or American Lake South) and Lake City to provide local news reports from those areas. While metropolitan papers such as the *Tacoma Daily Ledger* and the *Tacoma News Tribune* reported news for the area since the 1880s, the *Log* can be considered an early history book about this area.

Some of those contributions include the following examples from the 1937 to 1939 editions:

> *LAKE CITY NEWS, by Jeannette Lee* [from the December 3, 1937 issue]
> *Mrs. Mary Tate, principal of Lake City School, was pleasantly surprised on Nov. 29 when pupils of her room gave her a party honoring her birthday. The tables in the lunchroom were attractively decorated. Jello, with whipped cream, punch, ice cream and birthday cake were thoroughly enjoyed. The girls planned the party, and the boys helped them enjoy the eats. Mrs. Tate was presented with a gift.*
>
> *American Lake South Improvement Club (Tillicum) met last Monday. The list of officers for the new year include: Erick Johnson, President; Albert McArthur, Vice President; and Preston Mosper, Sec.-Treas.*

The club is hosting a Keno Night, with prizes worth everyone's time and money, of course, on Friday, Dec. 17.

Lakeside Country Club, by Mildred Fowler
Mr. and Mrs. Joe Baker were sponsors at a fraternity dance at the clubhouse on Friday night. The group had an enjoyable time, with a late supper ending the evening.

Mrs. E. P. Wilson has been detained in Longview, while she has been visiting her daughter, because of illness. She will be home soon, to take up her normal duties.

South American Lake, by Wallace Webber
Mr. and Mrs. Vernon R. Drinkwine and their guests Miss Amy Clarke and Warren Cowell have just returned from an enjoyable motor trip to San Francisco and Los Angeles.

Lake City, Jan. 1938
Mr. and Mrs. Joseph Holt were hosts to dinner for Rev. and Mrs. Edward Coy and family on Sunday.

We are sorry to see Jack Franklin still on crutches. Jack broke his leg four months ago.

South American Lake
Gladys Soomes, daughter of Mr. and Mrs. T. V. Soomes, of Seattle and formerly of Tillicum, married Charles Baraga in Seattle. They will make their home in San Francisco.

Lake City, by Luanne-Jean Judd
There was a skating party held in the evening. Mrs. Lee was in charge of the evening.

The American Lake South Community Club met last Wednesday evening with a large group turning out. In the membership drive that has been going on between the men and women; it was won by the men, therefore the ladies find that they will have to host the next dinner.

Tillicum, May 5, 1939
Bona's Market Remodels
The American Lake South Market has three free baskets of groceries and free Balloons to give away on Saturday.

> *Because of all the improvements in shelving and signage "even a near-sighted person could shop at the store and not miss a thing."*
>
> *Bona's store was located on the north end of today's Harry Todd Park.*
>
> *Specials at the store that week included: Nalley's Mayonnaise for $.39/jar, Dry, picked fryers for $.39/each, Pacific Brand, slightly salty crackers $.15 for a two-lb. caddy, and $.19 for three tall cans of Carnation Milk.*
>
> *Betty Grow reported that Girl Scout Troop 47 had taken a tour of American Lake Hospital where Dr. Stalter, Head of the hospital, gave the tour.*

The December 17, 1937 edition published complete details of Christmas programs of all area schools, including Lake City School.

Assorted Lake City and Tillicum Residents

Many prominent Tacoma residents took advantage of the opportunity to buy property around American Lake. Here are a few of early day and present residents.

Shortly after Lakeside Country Club was established, renowned Tacoma architect Ambrose Russell and his family built a small cabin adjacent to the country club property. Margaret Russell and her brother, James, attended the Lake City Elementary School, which Ambrose designed. The school was dedicated in 1914. At present, the school's fate is undetermined since within two years the elementary school's operation will be moving to Clover Park Technical College, where it will be incorporated into the new Harrison Preparatory School program.

James Sargent Russell, son of Ambrose and Lola Russell, was born in Tacoma on March 22, 1903. When Jim was four, the Russells bought an acre and a half on American Lake. They spent summers in the wooden-sided tent with a canvas roof until they were able to build a cabin. Ambrose was a renowned Tacoma architect who, among his many projects, designed Immanuel Presbyterian Church, the Tacoma Armory, Sunrise Lodge at Mount Rainier and the Perkins Building. In 1916, he designed Lake City Elementary School, which Jim and his sister, Margaret, attended.

During these summer outings at the lake, young James met a retired ship's carpenter, Mr. Nordeen. Nordeen became a role model for James, and time spent in his company ultimately influenced James's interest in a naval career.

He studied the lake's winds and currents as he sailed around it.

After attending DeKoven Hall, James went to Stadium High School and then signed on as a merchant marine because he was too young to enlist in the navy. The Russell homestead on American Lake remains in the family today. During World War II, James rose in rank to become an admiral. His life is chronicled in a separate book. Today, the aquatic center at Patriot's Landing at DuPont (a military retirement center) has been named for Admiral Russell. Russell Landing at Camp Murray, setting for the Evergreen Bass Club's annual Warrior's Fishing Derby, also is named for him.

SHARON MONTGOMERY, a Lakeside country club resident who lives in a 1908 home built there, said that the Russell family allowed country club residents to use water from their well for several years after the property was platted. In 2010, Sharon took on the role of club historian, compiling data for the club's centennial.

GLORIA BLAIR'S recollections include one about swimming across American Lake one summer day. Although her less-adventurous swimming partner turned back, Gloria kept swimming. A boat was finally sent out to pick her up, but, she says, she was reluctant to get into it because there were "so many people in it." She finally did climb inside the boat, though, and returned to shore.

Then there was the dance hall (possibly the Lake City Hotel that was built to accommodate guests who came to enjoy the lake) located at American Lake Park (where the parking lot now stands).

Gloria Blair's daughter, DIANA KIRBY, shared her recollections about growing up in Lake City. A sense of "feeling safe" permeated Diana's memories. A graduate of Lakes High School, after attending Lake City Elementary and Mann Middle School, she recalled coming to the church for cookies after school; the many church and school activities, such as shopping at the Holt Variety Store on Veteran's Drive; and walking to Steilacoom for a soda at the Bair Store. Now retired from Custer Elementary School, where the primary wing was named in her honor, Diana remains active in the Lake City Community Church and activities in the community where she was raised.

The Friedmans on the Lake

In notes provided by Deborah Friedman, Mr. Blaine purchased the American Lake Park lots from George W. Block on August 30, 1889. There was a hearing about the transaction held on June 18, 1890.

Block had purchased the property from Washington Territory in November 1871. He paid the standard $1.25 per acre for a parcel of 159 and 30/100 acres. His purchase price was $199 and twelve and a half cents.

Later that year, Adolph Friedman and four partners laid out streets and platted the areas of American Lake Park. His partners were Joseph and Ida Blaine and Jonathan and Martha Beardsley. (Blaine had married Ida Harkness in Tacoma on December 16, 1888. Apparently, both Beardsley and Blaine were prior landowners. In April 1884, Beardsley had paid ten dollars and filed a land patent on 160 acres on the other side of American Lake on what is now the Hillside area of Fort Lewis. The land was never developed.

The platted area was located on the west side of American Lake, just south of what is now the VA Hospital. It contained a beach on the southeast and an open prairie on the west and enclosed two small lakes. The street names included Friedman, Harkness, Prairie, Breeden, Marvin, Beherall, Lowenstein, Kapus and Beardsley.

"On and after Sept. 1, 1889, lots in Lake City, W.T., will be withdrawn from the market," the Friedman records note.

The Steam Plant Operator's Son

As a young boy growing up in Lake City, Art Herstrom's big ambition was to work in the steam plant at the newly opened Veterans' Administration Hospital—after all, what could be cooler than getting a job at the place where his father worked.

Art was born at St. Joseph's Hospital in Tacoma on July 4, 1925, to the Port Townsend/Cheney couple. For many years thereafter, Art thought that the nationwide, mid-summer celebration with parades and picnics was held in his honor.

Although he knows better now, his family continues to host a big bash on that date at the family home in Steilacoom. Art muses that the significant date may have influenced his career choice in later years when he became a radio operator on a B-29, serving in Korea after being on active duty during World War II.

Art's earliest recollection of the city by the largest of the Lakes District's dozen lakes was of living in a small cottage, "the second house from the corner," owned by Naomilawn and Dolly Madison. His family settled in a small home in Lake City. He spent a lot of time fishing on American Lake with his dad and picnicking on the island, especially one they called "Poison

Oak Island," since his mother contracted poison oak after they went there one time.

He recalled that he got good at launching boats on the Lake City side and often would beat the seaplane out of Martin's Boathouse on the lake (the forerunner of White's and, finally, McMahon's Seaplane Base).

Art recalled the vacant field in Lake City near an auto court. He said he swam and boated from Mrs. Thomas's beach and that she also operated the auto court area where they played football. They were so good that a report of one of their games made the news in the 1930s. In between boating and football, Art earned his Eagle Scout rank in Boy Scouts. Colonial Center builder Norton Clapp had been his scoutmaster at Little Church on the Prairie; all the men of Herstrom's family have attained Eagle Scout rank, he added.

Until his brother, Frank, arrived four and a half years later, Art enjoyed his status as an only child.

While he never did work in the VA Hospital's steam plant, after serving in the air force during the Korean War, he worked for Tacoma City Light Company from 1949 to 1988 (with three years at Boeing) as an engineer. He says he was a "60-cycle" man—that was the operating system then (nowadays it's computers).

Art had a "girlfriend" in first grade. But she was well-to-do, so that relationship didn't last long; she was promoted a grade ahead and always was ahead of him from then on.

His memories of Lake City include working first at Howard Aljo's store and then, as he grew older, as a stock clerk. He said there was a brand of Nabisco cookies—cake base, marshmallow and then a chocolate coating—that he especially liked. Art said he would arrange the cookies on the shelf so he'd always have access to his favorite variety. When he turned sixteen and was able to drive, he worked as delivery boy for Mr. Perati, who operated the store where Washington Boulevard and Interlaaken intersect. He earned $3.50 a week—"more for the experience than money." Art then worked for Pacific Fruit and Produce in Tacoma down on Dock Street. He'd ride the bus home to Avenue DuBois, where his family then lived. Because he arrived home late at night, the driver would wake him when it was time to get off the bus.

Art's favorite subjects included physics and math. His least favorite subject was history. Art eventually earned a degree in electrical engineering from the University of Washington and then an advanced degree from Stanford University in California. In 1946, the Holt Chapel was the setting for his marriage to Virginia. Her dad also worked at the VA Hospital, and the couple had three children.

He served in the U.S. Air Force during World War II (he trained in Texas, California and Florida) and then in Korea. He was a radio operator but wanted to be a pilot on a B-29.

Bailing out of B-29 after two of the engines failed during a bombing run was "quite an experience." All the men escaped uninjured, although one broke his leg and another was shot at when he was mistaken for an enemy as they landed near a South Korean base. The searchers were carrying torches—it was reminiscent of a scene from *Lost Horizons*.

During his schooling years, and while being assigned to different bases (Topeka, Palo Alto), he and his wife purchased and lived in a small trailer.

Art and Virginia moved to Steilacoom in 1991. They lived on property that was owned by Virginia's parents, who owned the corner lot. Art and his late wife planted a garden. Their back deck was a favorite gathering spot for family reunions—especially on the Fourth of July—with a good view of the sound and ferry terminal.

Art stays fit by taking daily walks around the town on the sound and enjoying the camaraderie of his men's Friday morning coffee group.

In a May 16, 2014 telephone interview with GARY TISSOT, formerly of Lake City, Tillicum and American Lake South but who now lives in Edmonds, Washington, he spoke at length about his recollections of growing up on the lake, such as playing on the pond behind Thornewood "Manor," as it was known in the days of the Stones' residence:

> *Gen. and Mrs. Stone wore long grey coats, and they stood in the back yard watching us* [local] *children play…At Hallowe'en it was spooky to visit the manor, but Mrs. Stone welcomed us inside the great hall and gave us treats…We used to play in the boathouse behind the "Manor."*

He also recalled exploring what were rumored to have been remains of the Hudson's Bay Company's Puget Sound Agricultural Company buildings (American Lake Gardens), but all that rubble was pushed into a small lake and covered over as fill.

His grandmother worked at the American Lake Inn, the original Lake City Hotel, in its days as a speakeasy, but by the time of the interview, the hotel was deteriorating.

Mr. Tissot continued, explaining that "no one in those Tillicum days knew who 'Harry Todd' was." (The park that now bears Todd's name was known as Bona's and named for the store owner.)

Mr. Tissot later attended University of Washington and then joined the navy. He also is a historian.

JACK AVRIL, another former Lake City resident, lived on Francis Folsom Road, not far from the lake's edge. Jack attended Lake City Elementary and then Clover Park High School, where he played for the Warriors. He later attended the University of Washington and became a private fire investigator. He met and married his wife, Janice, who was a nursing student at Seattle Pacific University.

The couple met during her summer internship at the VA Hospital in Lake City (he took her rowing on the lake), and a year later, they were married. Jack and Janice both were baptized at Lake City Church

Years later, he and two other CPHS grads founded the Ancient Warriors—a group of CPHS grads from classes of 1947 to '50 who met twice a week at Carr's but recently moved to Meadowpark Golf Course Grill.

On the day of the interview, Jack, his wife and I visited his former home. While the Avril home's current tenant showed her unexpected visitors around, Jack shared stories about his father, Jack Avril, who did much of the house's construction.

Standout memories, Jack said, were walking "up the hill from the house to the school," math classes and how "quiet it was" in Lake City—always a suburb of Lakewood.

Although Jack's memories are growing fainter, he enjoys the Tuesday morning breakfast gatherings at Meadowpark Golf Course Grill.

PEGGY MACE BALL is the granddaughter of A.J. Russell. She passed away in March 2014. (Margaret Russell was Peggy's mother. Peggy's father was Dr. Norman Mace.)

"I spent the first eleven years of my life in a mental hospital," Peggy says

Before one gasps and says, "Well, she certainly seems OK to me," Peggy explains that her father, Dr. Norman Mace, was a psychiatrist at the Veterans' Hospital on American Lake near Tacoma, Washington.

The Maces lived on Doctors' Row with a beautiful rose garden at one end. Peggy commented that the hospital "did promise us a rose garden."

> *There was a hedge separating us from the rest of the beautiful grounds at the other. When my sister and I went beyond the hedge, it was a switch from this hedge wielded by our mother against the backs of our legs that brought us back. The houses were white stucco, with red tile roofs like the rest of the buildings at the hospital. We had a lovely lawn in front of the row, with tall fir trees. It sloped down to the lake, where we learned to swim at an early age.*
>
> *The grounds were kept up by the patients, and we weren't afraid of them. Of course, only the nonviolent men were allowed this privilege. They were all old men, or seemed so to us. Since World War II hadn't started yet, most of them were veterans of the Spanish-American War or the First World War.*
>
> *We became well acquainted with several patients. I remember one man especially. His name was Hoolihan. We'd sit on the grass and talk for hours. He always told me he was going to the fair, where he would get me either a diamond ring or an emerald bracelet. I spent a lot of time trying to decide which one I wanted, but I think I always knew I wasn't going to get either.*
>
> *A favorite saying of Hoolihan's was: "Dinner is just like the movies. You never know what it's going to be until you get there."*

Living at the hospital was a very good life for the Mace girls, Peggy adds. They didn't learn until later that mental illness is frightening or that having a mental hospital in the neighborhood can lower property values.

> *We didn't know you have to watch what you say to a mental patient. Maybe if everyone treated the mentally ill just like other people, the way the very young do, there would be less mental illness and an easier and faster recovery for them.*

Carol Moreno attended Lake City Elementary School and then graduated from Stadium High School in Tacoma. A very colorful memory from her early Lake City days (she still lives in Lake City) focuses on the day she and a friend bought surplus World War II battleship gray paint from the navy surplus store where Clover Park Technical College now stands. The plan was to paint her bedroom walls purple. Carol remembers they made several trials with the paint before achieving the right shade of purple she wanted. The girls finally achieved the right shade by mixing in several tubes of lipstick. The almost fatal result, though, was they'd forgotten to open the bedroom windows while painting!

Highlights from her Lake City growing-up days include the late '40s and early '50s, when the lake froze.

Carol had an acquaintance who played the concert harp. The girl's father purchased a Nash Rambler (with fold-down seats in which to transport the harp to various concert sites.

Wilbur Barker still lived at the family homestead at the intersection of Gravelly Lake Drive and Veteran's Drive, where the family owned a six-acre farm. Barker, who graduated in 1941 from Clover Park High School (according to the 1942 Clover Park High School yearbook, Barker's nickname was "Squeeky"), says that the farm supplied Lakeside Country Club residents with produce.

Wilbur Barker, whose parents operated a farm in Lake City. *Author's collection.*

Lisa Boyd, Lake City Elementary School principal, is looking forward to the 2015 move to Clover Park Technical College, where she'll administer the Harrison Preparatory School that's being readied for its official opening that year. Development of this school district/technical college partnership began when Lakewood's first mayor, Lieutenant General Bill Harrison (U.S. Army, retired) proposed the program for the Lake City Elementary School. Since 2010, the plan has been for middle school students (grades six through ten) to follow an International Baccalaureate curriculum, advancing into the district's IB school at Clover Park Technical College. Plans for the existing Lake City Elementary School have not yet been finalized.

Tim Marsh, whose father, Robert Marsh, was chief dental officer at American Lake Veterans' Administration Hospital, said that his family had just moved to Quarters 13B at American Lake VA when the October 1962 Columbus Day storm hit. Tim's father was out of state, receiving training at Fort Sam Houston in Texas. Tim's sister, Mayo, a student who was at that time attending the University of Oregon, phoned to let her mother know that she was "all right." "All right about what?" her mother asked. The wind and devastation experienced in Oregon would affect the American Lake hospital facilities and grounds later that day. Tall trees, which fell across the road in front of the doctors' quarters, were cut with chainsaws and removed.

Lifelong Tillicum resident JAMES TAYLOR, a local building contractor, also serves on the Tillicum Neighborhood Advisory Committee and the board of Lakewood Historical Society. He's also a proud member of the Ancient Warriors of Clover Park. Besides Ed and Bob Firch, the three men are considered "lifetime" residents of the community since they've lived there since they were born, and they take pride in that fact. Jim first attended Tillicum School in the 1940s, after it first was built; graduated from Clover Park High School in 1950; and, in later years, did subsequent repairs on the structure.

Jim was responsible for collecting and preparing materials that were included in the Tillicum Centennial Scrapbook. He planned to turn that information into a book for community residents. Later, Jim loaned that material for this history book project, and much of it has since been incorporated into *American Lake Vignettes*. Thanks go to Jim for numerous newspaper articles, photos and personal anecdotes about life in Tillicum.

OTHER AMERICAN LAKE COMMUNITIES

Camp Murray, Woodbrook Hunt Club, Tacoma Country and Golf Club

Camp Murray, Woodbrook Hunt Club and Tacoma Country and Golf Cub are three American Lake communities worthy of note. Although they are not "on the lake," they are close enough to be included in this work. Camp Murray, directly south of Tillicum, abuts the VA Hospital.

Access through Tillicum to Camp Murray has been a "sticky" issue among Tillicum residents due to the heavy increase in traffic since 2000.

CAMP MURRAY was not formally established until 1889, predating Fort Lewis by a generation. It was in use in 1855 as a spot for military training during the Indian War. It became a National Guard state headquarters in 1922. The name "Camp Murray" commemorates the Murray party that originally settled the area.

Guardsmen assigned there have seen a wide range of missions, such as disaster relief efforts, the Mexican border campaign against Pancho Villa, both world wars, the Korean War, the Berlin crisis, the Vietnam War, the eruption of Mount St. Helens in 1980 and, most recently, the operations in Afghanistan and Iraq.

WOODBROOK HUNT CLUB (WHC) is a ninety-eight-year-old organization, dedicated to riding with hounds (the custom involves costumed riders pursuing a fox, accompanied by other riders and their hunting dogs), a pursuit that extends back to the time well before George Washington hunted with his own pack of hounds in colonial Virginia. WHC is the oldest fox hunting club west of the Mississippi. The club today continues its rich tradition on the last remaining 3 percent of native prairie in the Puget Sound corridor.

Woodbrook is one of 170 member hunts of the Masters of Foxhounds Association of America (MFHA). The MFHA's keeper of the stud book maintains the pedigrees of its foxhounds. The hunt club has existed so long because of the military reservation at Fort Lewis, which its members are allowed to use (in common with the public and other groups) pursuant to a permit system and a licensing agreement through the Army Corps of Engineers.

The riders are not only grateful to but also dependent on the U.S. Army for its sport. All who ride with the club must sign a release of liability that excludes Fort Lewis and the Hunt (the Washington Hunt Club) from responsibility for any mishap that might occur during the risky business of riding and galloping across a country whose primary use is military training. There are definitely hazards, including the dreaded concertina wire, which make it wise to ride in the track of another rider.

TACOMA COUNTRY AND GOLF CLUB (TC&GC, established 1894) is located at the north end of American Lake and is the oldest country club "west of the Mississippi."

However, it wasn't until 1905 that the first clubhouse on American Lake was built. Approximately 250 people attended the June 25, 1905 opening, with special chartered Northern Pacific trains transporting the guests to and from town "for the festive occasion."

This enclosed community with its eighteen-hole course has occupied three structures on the lake site. The first two were destroyed by fire; the first fire took place on June 22, 1909.

Tacoma architect Ambrose Russell, who designed many area buildings, including the Perkins Building, the Washington Armory, the governor's mansion and Lake City Elementary School, designed the club's second headquarters, still referred to as the "Grand Old Lady." The second clubhouse burned on December 21, 1961.

"The first golf course layout at the American Lake site was quite primitive by any standard due to the limited amount of funds available because the Club House was the first priority," Shirlee Smith's 1994 history book for the club's centennial notes. Chester Thorne was club president in 1906.

That year, the Tacoma Railway and Power Company expanded to run a spur track into the club grounds, near the twelfth hole, and the Grays Harbor Branch of Northern Pacific built a small station approximately opposite the eighth green.

Because of the proximity of Camp Lewis (now Joint Base Lewis-McChord), it was inevitable that World War I impacted the TC&GC. Special "wheatless" and "porkless" meals became part of the routine in those years. Social activities, such as a Red Cross golf tournament, which raised about seventy-five dollars, was one World War I event held there.

According to Shirlee Smith:

> *Situated on the outskirts of the City of Tacoma from which electric cars run to links every half hour Tacoma's Country and Golf Club (organized 1894), has a Membership of 130. The Entrance Fee is $10, and Annual Dues are $6. The 18 hole-course was laid out in December 1894…visiting golfers are welcome to come use the course gratis on all ordinary days. The women players have a branch to themselves and elect their own officers, though they use the same course as the men.*

The TC&GC is accessible from Gravelly Lake Drive, en route to I-5, and anchors the northeastern end of American Lake between Lake City and Tillicum.

Chapter 7

WHAT'S AHEAD FOR AMERICAN LAKE

THE FUTURE?

For twenty years (1851–71), the town of Steilacoom also served as the location for the Pierce County Courthouse. After the county commissioners relocated the courthouse to the city of Tacoma, they began overseeing all county-related matters. Because of that temporary dual jurisdiction, the town has two sets of minute books.

It wasn't until 1871 that the town of Steilacoom elected its first mayor, William Wallace, who also served one term as territorial governor of Idaho.

Between 1871 and 1995, the Pierce County Council governed unincorporated communities, such as Lake City and Tillicum. The original Pierce County board of county commissioners was based in Steilacoom at the courthouse located on Gove Street. (That also briefly served as the location for Steilacoom's early school.)

After Lakewood and several other communities were voted in as cities in the 1990s, Lakewood took over jurisdiction of unincorporated areas such as Lakeview and the International District.

Prior to incorporation, according to Jim Taylor, a lifelong resident of the Tillicum community, the main issues of concern to residents in the small community on the east side of American Lake were crime, traffic, growth and planning, taxes and incorporation.

Residents weren't the ones committing the crimes, Taylor said. In the late 1980s, there was a sheriff's precinct set up to deal with those issues. It closed after three years. Now the City of Lakewood handles those matters. At the time of this writing, "Tillicum has the lowest crime rate of any neighborhood in the city," Taylor said.

One early 1980s newspaper story reported about a confrontation between residents and soldiers from nearby Fort Lewis, who complained that "there wasn't anything to do."

Shortly after that story was published, Pierce County built a community center to provide activities and services.

Later, the newly incorporated City of Lakewood began imposing strict rules and regulations on the rural area. Requiring residents to connect to sewer lines was one major issue that was resisted.

Three years before cityhood for Lakewood, a news story told about Tillicum being advised that "cityhood costs more money" In a November 1993 story, Pierce County council members told Tillicum's incorporation supporters that they "had better make sure there was enough money to 'run a municipality.'"

According to county guidelines, any area hoping to incorporate had to have at least 3,000 residents. At the time of that article, Tillicum had only 2,600 residents.

Former Lakewood mayor Doug Richardson today represents Lake City and Tillicum on the Pierce County council. Lakewood council member John Simpson, a Pierce College–Fort Steilacoom history teacher, represents Tillicum, while Lakewood council member Paul Bocchi, a budget legislative analyst with the Pierce County Council, represents Lake City. In the early years of Lakewood's incorporation, the city embarked on a plan to improve the lake's condition by making residents connect to a sewer system. Connecting to the sewer system was a financial hardship for many Tillicum residents until arrangements were made to help them pay for the connections.

Also, Habitat for Humanity began a building project there, with fifteen new "affordable" homes to be built during the next few months.

In the late 1980s, many of Pierce County's unincorporated areas, such as Lakewood, University Place, Milton and Edgewood, were encouraged to form their own local governments, Not all of these areas gained city status. Outlying unincorporated communities such as Lake City, Lakeview and Tillicum were designated as "neighborhoods" and placed under the City of Lakewood's jurisdiction.

Although a concise understanding of this subject warrants a separate book, this serves as a brief overview of that situation.

What lies ahead for the communities of Tillicum and Lake City?

While the communities were relegated to "neighborhood" status in 1996, residents in those areas (which have Lakewood councilmembers assigned to conduct monthly update meetings for their areas) are confident, although detached, about how the city governs them. The city distributes a quarterly newsletter called *Community Connections*, informing residents about activities impacting their neighborhoods.

A Final Word from Louis about American Lake

April 26, 2014, was the official opening day for fishing on American Lake. Hundreds of fishermen launched their boats and cast their lines in hopes of catching the rainbow trout that had been released earlier that week. American Lake is considered the premier fishing lake in Pierce County. The lake also contains yellow perch, large and small mouth bass and Kokanee. As author Louis Raphael attests, "There's nothing like spending the day in a boat, rowing around the lake."

Dave Anderson (of Bill's Boathouse) and his son-in-law, Mike Barr, today continue a tradition begun by Dave's dad, Glenn, in the 1990s. Although the State of Washington periodically stocks the lake, Bill's Boathouse assists by nurturing some more than six thousand rainbows each year. Once the holding pen (consisting of a holding net and cover net), along with the pen frame, is put together each fall, the boathouse team feeds the young fish an average of fifty pounds per day for three days a week.

"The fish," David says, "are generally released the third week of April the following year. For the most part, the trout that originally weighed between three to four ounces each now weigh about a pound."

Without a doubt, Louis knows well the pleasures of lake fishing:

> *As near as I can figure, I started fishing in American Lake in 1942 and fished there at least once every year through 2005. Some of my friends have been married nearly that long—and to one person! But I got along with the lake better than any woman I ever knew, even though I felt it was trying to drown me a time or two.*
>
> *After all these years, American Lake is still the lake of my dreams. If it were any better it would be too perfect.*

What a break to have such an experience during my formative years. Those days on our big raft of a dock must surely have rivaled those of Mark Twain's characters on the Mississippi.

I still dream from time to time of fishing with Jim or alone. The lake is American, and I know they're in there. I am always hoping to feel once more that pulsing on my rod that pleases so much. You might even say I got a few.

Washington's Two Lake Cities

The Puget Sound region has many lakes with communities built on their shores, but according to an Internet search, only two Washington State cities have the official name of "Lake City."

Lake City North is located about eight miles north of Seattle, while Lake City South is located about the same distance from Tacoma. An Internet search turned up thirteen other U.S. communities named "Lake City."

Washington's Lake Cities began at approximately the same time (1854), when Native American tribes (Duwamish, Lushootseed, Nisqually and Steilacoom) established permanent settlements after ice from the last glacial period receded.

The Lake City located on the shore of Lake Washington has become the more prominent of the two, with Lake City North having the earlier claim. The northern Lake City area was clear cut by a crude wagon road or by using Lake Washington, from 1850 past the turn of the century; more rapidly with the Seattle, Lake Shore and Eastern Railway (around 1886) providing easy access along what is now the Burke-Gilman Trail adjacent to the lake. Wetlands were drained. A Little Germany neighborhood of several immigrant farmers grew up in the 1870s around where Nathan Hale High School now stands.

Lake City resident Imogene Inglit has published a short history of that community this past January, entitled *Lil' Ol' Lake City*. With her permission, we turn to that work here, in part, to explain how the city got its name.

That northerly Lake City, according to its chamber of commerce archives, once was called Pontiac, at one time a hamlet that depended on a brickyard on the shores of Lake Washington for its livelihood. There were plenty of fields and woods, and children had only to choose which swimming hole they wanted. As the settlement grew away from the lake into the uplands, it became known as Cedar Park.

The origins of the name "Lake City" come from an incident when Northern Pacific Railroad workers hung the name "Lake" on a shed near the tracks. People living nearby adopted the name and tagged on "City."

The story adds, "Welcome to Lake City, The Gateway to Seattle, where friendliness is the No. 1 priority."

Lake City South, on the west shore of American Lake, wasn't formally established until 1889, when Tacoma Land Company promoted the area for home sites. Any dream of cityhood was abandoned after the Panic of 1893, when many Tacoma and Steilacoom speculators lost money.

Celebrations around American Lake

Lakeside communities, from Silcox Island (2005) to Lakeside Country Club and Tillicum (2010), have marked their centennial years with special celebrations. This year, Lake City shares its 125th anniversary (May 1, 1889) with Washington State. Still to come is a centennial celebration for the American Lake Veterans' Affairs Hospital in 2024.

Although Washington Territory did not officially become a state until November 11, 1889, and Lake City never became a city, because they share the milestone founding year, plans are underway to celebrate that shared occasion in 2014. A display focusing on Lake City historical materials is scheduled for this summer, while numerous 125th/statehood community events around the state are presently being planned for the state's celebration. It is hoped that Lake City's 125th will be recognized as part of Washington State's 125th anniversary this year.

Small-Town Benefits

America has become an overwhelmingly metropolitan nation. According to the 2000 census, more than 80 percent of the nation's population resides in one of the 350 combined metropolitan statistical areas. It is not surprising, therefore, that small-town America might be considered to be becoming a burdensome anachronism.

Nothing could be further from the truth, according to one report on the Internet. America is more "small town" than we often think, particularly in how we govern ourselves. At the start of the twenty-first century, slightly more than half of the nation's population lived in jurisdictions (meaning cities, towns, boroughs, villages and townships), with fewer than twenty-five thousand people in rural areas. Planners and geographers might see regions as mega-units, but in fact they are usually composed of many small towns and far fewer larger cities. Among the metropolitan areas that had more than one million residents at the turn of the twenty-first century, the average-sized city, town, borough, village or township had a population of little more than twenty thousand residents; five thousand fewer than the twenty-five-thousand-person benchmark cited above.

America's small-town government structure engenders a sense of community, even as part of larger metropolitan areas. It also saves a lot of money, principally because democracy tends to work better when government is closer to home. It is not surprising that so many consolidation proposals fail, and that, when given the chance, voters usually reject consolidation proposals.

America needs both its small towns and its bigger cities. But make no mistake about it, even much of what we call a "metropolis" functions more effectively as a network of small towns.

What Attracts Residents to the Lake?

Longtime residents Liz Parkinson and Jim Taylor, from opposite sides of American Lake, reflect about what it means to live in this area.

Liz Parkinson

> *Every spring and summer, I experience déjà vu, and I return to the life in Lake City when I was growing up. My parents and I moved to Lake City in 1953 from North Dakota, and after all these years, I still hear frogs croaking at night, smell the sweet air and see sparkling water on American Lake. I think that many have enjoyed these treats to their senses as I have, and it is timeless, going back to the first people who were here.*

Winter sunset view of American Lake. *Tacoma Public Library.*

Jim Taylor

I was born and raised in Tillicum and have lived here all of my life. During the 1950s and '60s we did live on American Lake. Living on the lake was a fantastic experience. It brought swimming, boating, fishing and water skiing right up to our door. This was really special, as we were raising our children during this time. To this day, they talk about their experiences and how happy they were growing up with the opportunities that living on the lake provided for them.

Over the years, the quality of life in Tillicum has had its ups and downs. However, during the time from about the mid-1980s to the present time, the quality if life has gradually improved to the point where we now have a very safe and quiet community in which to live.

I attribute a lot of that success to the assistance that came from Pierce County (before Lakewood became a city), by the construction of the Community Center and the placement of a library in the center. They also improved our streets and installed sidewalks on most of them to improve the safety of our residents.

After Lakewood became a city, we also received sewers on the major streets with further improvements for pedestrian safety. Along with this, Habitat for Humanity is now building some thirty new homes in Tillicum. What all of this has done is to prompt many of the homeowners who have homes for rent to make improvements to their properties. Tillicum now has the lowest crime rate of any neighborhood in the City of Lakewood.

Irish poet William Butler Yeats summarizes his thoughts about lake living in his poem "The Lake Isle at Innisfree." The words are applicable to American Lake:

I will arise and go now, for always night and day
I hear lake water lapping with low sounds by the shore;
While I stand on the roadway, or on the pavement gray,
I hear it in the deep heart's core.

AFTERWORD

History is not static; it's always evolving. If a book were able to keep up with the topic, it could never be published. It is hoped, though, that *American Lake Vignettes* has sparked an interest and that its readers will be inspired to further research the many stories about the place once promoted as Tacoma's playground.

RESOURCES

Anderson, David. Interview with author, 2013.

———. *Tillicum/Woodbrook Neighborhood Association Newsletter*, March 2014. [This monthly e-mailed newsletter contains a report to residents about events, activities and other happenings that affect them.]

Archambault, Alan. *The History of Fort Lewis*. Charleston, SC: Arcadia Publishing, 2002.

Avril, Jack. Interview with author, 2013.

Bal, Peggy Mace. *The Memoirs of Peggy Mace Bal*. N.p.: self-published, 1960s.

Barker, Wilbur. Interview with author, 2013.

Bill's Boathouse History. Collected by David Anderson, Tillicum Neighborhood Association.

Blair, Gloria. Interview with author, 2013.

Bonney. W.P. *History of Pierce County*. Chicago: Pioneer Historical Publishing Company, 1927.

Brown, Daniel James. *The Boys in the Boat*. New York: Viking, 2012.

Dunkelberger, Steve. "Tacoma Trolleys, 1890–1930." HistoryLink.org. http://www.historylink.org/index.cfm?DisplayPage=output.cfm&file_id=5640.

Elphendahl, Gerry. Interview with author, 2013.

Forman, Maury, and Rick Marshall, eds. *Cartooning Washington: 100 Years of Cartoon Art in Washington State*. N.p.: Melior, 1989.

Friedman, Deb. Interview with author, 2013.

———. Personal correspondence with author, 2013.

Gallopin' with Gertie. Monthly publication of Gertie's Restaurant, Tillicum.

Gierke, Susan, comp. Silcox Island's 2005 Centennial Book. 2010.

Heath, Joseph. *Memoirs of Nisqually—1847*. Fairfield, WA: Ye Galleon Press, 1979.

Herstrom, Art. Interview with author, 2013.

Holm, Clary, comp. Assorted Tillicum and Lake City documents. Tacoma Public Library.

Hunt, Herbert. *Tacoma, Its History and Its Builders: A Half Century of Activity*. Chicago: S.J. Clarke, 1916.

Inglit, Imogene. Phone interview with Lake City, Seattle resident, June 2014.

Kauffman, Kris. Phone interview with author, June 2014.

Kauffman, Kris, and Don Russell. *Lakewood's Lakes District*. Program presented at Lakewood Historical Society, 2012.

Kirby, Diane. Interview with author, 2013.

———. *Lake City Community Church History*. Program presented at Lakewood Historical Society, 2010.

Krukeberg, Arthur R. *The Natural History of Puget Sound Country*. Seattle: University of Washington Press, 1991.

Lakeside Country Club Centennial History. N.p.: self-published, 2010.

Lakewood Log, 1937–39.

Maas, Virginia. *One Room and a Path.* Albuquerque, NM: Americana Publishing, 2001.

Mann, Charles. Publisher.

Marshall, Danny. *Steilacoom Tribal Newsletter* (Spring 2012). [A monthly publication of the Steilacoom Tribe, consisting of updates about current tribal projects.]

Marsh, Tim. "Columbus Day Storm Recollection," 2012.

Matthews, Henry C. *Kirtland Cutter, Architect in the Land of Promise*. Seattle: University of Washington Press, 1999.

Montgomery, Sharon. Interview with author, 2013.

Moreno, Carol. Interview with author, 2013.

Morgan, Murray. *Puget's Sound*. Seattle: University of Washington Press, 1979.

Parkinson, Elizabeth. Interview, "Lake City Reminiscences," May 2014.

Peterson, Dave. Interview with author, 2013.

Puget Sound Agricultural Company. Statistics at Fort Nisqually, Point Defiance Park, Tacoma, WA.

Raphael, Louis. *They're in There: A Life on American Lake*. N.p.: self-published, 2009.

Rechnitzer, Paul. "Four Sages: Interviews with Four Idaho Historians." *Sandpoint Magazine* (Winter 2014).

Reese, Gary, and Frank Jackson, comps. American Lake VA Hospital History. Tacoma Public Library.

Smith, Shirlee H. *The Tacoma Country and Golf Club, 1894*. N.p.: self-published, 1984.

Tacoma Chamber of Commerce. *Tacoma Illustrated.* Chicago: Baldwin, Calcutt and Co., 1889

Tacoma Daily Ledger, 1880s.

Tacoma News Tribune, 1909, 1924, 1960.

Taylor, Jim. Interview with author, 2013–14.

Wikipedia. "British Lake District." http://en.wikipedia.org/wiki/Lake_District.

———. "Great Northern Railway." http://en.wikipedia.org/wiki/Great_Northern_Railway_(U.S.).

———. "Mount Rainier." http://en.wikipedia.org/wiki/Mount_Rainier.

———. "Thornewood Castle." http://en.wikipedia.org/wiki/Thornewood.

INDEX

ABOUT THE AUTHOR

Courtesy of Jeff Wolff.

Nancy Covert, a retired Northwest community journalist, lived for two decades in Steilacoom, Washington State's first incorporated town, before relocating to Lake City, a small suburban neighborhood in the recently incorporated City of Lakewood (1996).

A native of Pennsylvania, Nancy moved west in the early 1960s. In the late 1970s, she embarked on her journalism career. Starting in Central Washington, she began writing for community publications in Washington and Idaho. At each paper where she worked, from the Puget Sound region to the Idaho Panhandle and back, the experiences added to her understanding and appreciation for small-town living.

In each community, she joined one of the region's historical societies, gaining access to further research materials, inspiring numerous articles.

After immersing herself in these fascinating histories about the various northwestern places where she lived, in 1991 she settled in the Town of

Steilacoom, the first incorporated town (1854) in Washington Territory, and became involved with many of the area's community celebrations.

"If you're going to move to a new place, it behooves you to get acquainted with where you are and learn to like it and become a part of the community," advised Idaho historian Paul Rechnitzer.

In 2011, she moved to Lake City, but she soon discovered there was no single source of information about her newest "hometown" community. Following the encouraging recommendation of another historian, this project was begun.

Nancy is co-author of *Mrs. Orr's Pear Tree*, *Steilacoom Historical School District #1: 150 Years of Educating Steilacoom Students* and *Women of Steilacoom*. She also is the author of several works of fiction, including *Kaniksu Magic*.

As part of her ongoing research for articles for the *Suburban Times*, a contemporary online publication to which she frequently contributes, Nancy regularly combs through archived copies of the *Log*, Lakewood's first newspaper, published from 1937 to 1961, for story ideas.

Besides *American Lake Vignettes*, Nancy has two books being prepared for publication: one about early Steilacoom, Washington newspapers (1855 and onward) and *Beachcombing with Scheherazade*, a compilation of *almost* 1,001 stories from her journalism career.